INSIGHT POCKET GUIDE

S0-BFA-568

PARIS

Discovery
CHANNEL

APA PUBLICATIONS
Part of the Langenscheidt Publishing Group

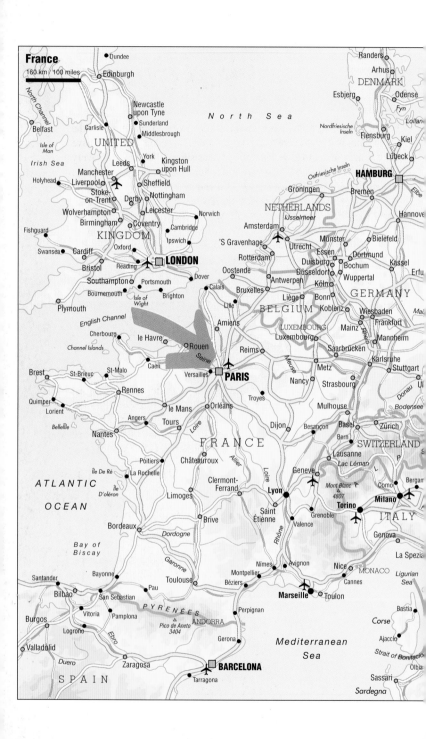

France

160 km / 100 miles

North Sea

North Channel

Dundee
Edinburgh
Newcastle
upon Tyne
Sunderland
Middlesbrough
Belfast
Carlisle
Isle of Man
Irish Sea
UNITED
York
Leeds
Kingston
upon Hull
Manchester
Liverpool
Holyhead
Sheffield
Stoke-
on-Trent
Derby
Nottingham
Wolverhampton
Leicester
Birmingham
Coventry
Norwich
Fishguard
KINGDOM
Cambridge
Oxford
Ipswich
Swansea
Cardiff
LONDON
Bristol
Reading
Southampton
Portsmouth
Bournemouth
Isle of Wight
Brighton
Plymouth
English Channel
Cherbourg
le Havre
Rouen
Channel Islands
Brest
St-Brieuc
St-Malo
Caen
Seine
Versailles
PARIS
Quimper
Rennes
Lorient
Belle Île
le Mans
Orléans
Troyes
Angers
Tours
Nantes
Loire
Châteauroux
Poitiers
Île De Ré
La Rochelle
Allier
ATLANTIC
Limoges
Clermont-
Ferrand
Île D'oléron
Loire
OCEAN
Brive
Bordeaux
Dordogne
Saint
Étienne
Bay of Biscay
Garonne
Nîmes
Santander
Bayonne
Pau
Toulouse
Montpellier
Béziers
Bilbao
San Sebastian
P Y R É N É E S
Perpignan
Burgos
Vitoria
Pamplona
Pico de Aneto
3404
ANDORRA
Logroño
Ebro
Gerona
*Mediterranean
Sea*
Valladolid
Duero
Zaragosa
BARCELONA
S P A I N
Tarragona

DENMARK
Randers
Arhus
Esbjerg
Odense
Fyn
Lolland
Nordfriesische Inseln
Flensburg
Kiel
Lübeck
Ostfriesische Inseln
HAMBURG
Elbe
Groningen
Bremen
Hannov
NETHERLANDS
Münster
Bielefeld
IJsselmeer
Amsterdam
Essen
Dortmund
'S Gravenhage
Utrecht
Duisburg
Bochum
Kassel
Rotterdam
Düsseldorf
Wuppertal
Erfu
Oostende
Antwerpen
Köln
GERMANY
Calais
Bruxelles
Liège
Bonn
Koblenz
Lille
BELGIUM
Wiesbaden
Amiens
Mai
LUXEMBOURG
Mainz
Frankfurt
Reims
Luxembourg
Mannheim
Saarbrücken
Metz
Karlsruhe
Nancy
Stuttgart
Strasbourg
Donau
Mulhouse
Bodensee
Dijon
Besançon
Basel
Zürich
Bern
SWITZERLAND
Lausanne
Geneve
Lac Léman
Lyon
Como
Bergan
Mont Blanc
4807
Torino
Milano
Grenoble
Valence
ITALY
Rhône
Genova
La Spezia
Avignon
Nice
MONACO
Ligurian Sea
Marseille
Cannes
Toulon
Bastia
Corse
Ajaccio
Strait of Bonifacio
Olbia
Sassari
Sardegna

F R A N C E

introduction

Welcome

This guidebook combines the interests and enthusiasms of two of the world's best-known information providers: Insight Guides, who have set the standard for visual travel guides since 1970, and Discovery Channel, the world's premier source of non-fiction television programming. Its aim is to show visitors the best of Paris and its surroundings in 15 carefully designed itineraries prepared by Insight's correspondent in Paris, Grace Coston. It begins with four full-day tours linking the main areas of interest, such as Notre Dame and the Latin Quarter, the Grand Boulevards, the Marais and Bastille areas, and western Paris, including the Eiffel Tower. These are followed by six more itineraries focusing on other interesting areas and aspects of the city from Père Lachaise cemetery to Montmartre, and then four excursions to Versailles, Chartres, Monet's water garden at Giverny and Disneyland Paris. Supporting the itineraries are sections on history and culture, shopping, eating out and nightlife, a calendar of special events and a fact-packed practical information section, which includes a list of recommended hotels.

Grace Coston, Insight's correspondent in Paris, works in the city as a writer, translator and teacher, and is also mother to bilingual children. 'Besides being arguably the best preserved and grandest city in the world,' she says, 'Paris is a major hub of intellectual, cultural and artistic achievement. In the words of G.K. Chesterton, "If a man fell out of the moon into the town of Paris he would know that it was the capital of a great nation".' Even after living in Paris for many years she is still discovering more about it every day. 'I can firmly say that I wouldn't live anywhere else, and my enthusiasm for the city is even greater than it was when I first arrived. This book is a way of showing off my home town,' says Grace. 'And any friend of Paris is a friend of mine.'

6   contents

contents 7

9 By Canal to La Villette takes you by boat under the *Bastille* and along canals to *Parc de la Villette*, home of the *City of Science and Industry*, a museum popular with children of all ages **58**

10 The New Louvre is a brief guide to this superb, recently reorganised museum **61**

11 La Défense is a highly recommended visit to this avant-garde business district situated on the west side of the city centre **65**

EXCURSIONS
1 Versailles visits the fabulous palace and gardens created by the Sun King Louis XIV **67**

2 Chartres travels by train to this relaxing city with one of the world's finest Gothic cathedrals **69**

3 Giverny explores Monet's home town and visits the gardens depicted in many of his paintings **70**

4 Disneyland Paris takes a trip to the world of Walt, for an experience both you and the kids will enjoy......**71**

LEISURE ACTIVITIES
In this back section of the book are ideas on what to buy and where to buy it, plus suggested places to eat, drink and be merry. A calendar of events lists what's going on throughout the Parisian year **73–85**

PRACTICAL INFORMATION
All the essential background information for your visit to Paris, from taxis to tipping, customs to consulates. Plus a list of recommended hotels....................................**87–97**

MAPS
France 4	*Bois to Eiffel* **40**
Paris **18–19**	*From Rodin to Dior* **46**
Notre Dame and the	*Père Lachaise*...............**48**
Left Bank..................**22**	*Shopping Tour* **51**
The Grand Boulevards .**28**	*Montmartre & Pigalle* .**54**
Marais and Bastille **34**	*Metro* **88**

INDEX AND CREDITS
pages **99–104**

Preceding pages: a celebrated café
Following pages: the view from Pont Alexandre III

CLOVIS I.

History & Culture

Long ago, Paris was a simple village of mud huts nestled on an island in the River Seine. At the far reaches of the Roman Empire, the city Lutetia, as the Romans called it, was a mere outpost until Julian built a palace for himself in AD358. Barbarians, Parisii boatmen (members of a Celtic tribe), and Romans fought frequently on the surrounding plain and all left their mark on the developing character of the Parisians.

Attila the Hun was an unwelcome visitor in the 5th century. The legend of St Geneviève, the patron saint of Paris, was created when she 'saved' the city from his men. Then only 19, she assured the citizens that the Huns would spare Paris, and when her forecast proved correct, a cult formed around her.

Clovis I brought his Frankish armies to Gaul shortly thereafter, defeating the Gallo-Romans at Soissons. He consolidated his power by beating the Alemanni tribe at Tolbiac in 496 and the Visigoths near Poitiers in 507. Clovis moved the capital to Paris and the Merovingian dynasty was underway. He built the Church of the Apostles to honour the remains of St Geneviève and was buried there himself. Now the Panthéon sits on the hill, the final resting place for distinguished citizens such as Victor Hugo and Rousseau.

A City Shaped

The Capetian dynasty, which began in 987 with Hugues Capet and finally fizzled out 806 years later with the execution of Louis XVI, ruled during a period of considerable growth. The city was improved with public fountains, paved streets, and armed police to maintain order. Paris was emerging as a major European city. All over the country, religious fervour inspired the building of some of France's most famous monuments such as Normandy's Mont-St-Michel.

Trade continued to boom throughout the 12th century. Merchants united in powerful guilds, controlling city finance and administration. King Philippe Auguste built a big covered market (Les Halles), improved the waterfront for trade and erected a great wall around the city.

The Church remained strong during the difficult Dark Ages and with prosperity grew stronger. In addition to Notre Dame, smaller churches arose in its Gothic likeness, and old Romanesque edifices were restored and rebuilt. Already a commercial and ecclesiastical centre, Paris also became the centre of scholarship in medieval Europe, and was the first of the great capitals to have a university. A meeting place for scholars and theologians, controversy and debate became part of the city's character, and remain so today.

The upstart scholar Pierre Abélard was the first to attract students to the Left Bank, where the universities of Paris and the Sorbonne would open

Left: Clovis I, king of the Franks, saw off the Romans
Above: a Celtic coin

(the latter named after Robert de Sorbon). Latin, used in lectures and debates, gave the neighbourhood the name it now bears, *Le Quartier Latin*, and it remains the city's student centre. The unfortunate Abélard, however, took attracting students too far, and was castrated and sent to a monastery for showing rather too much affection for one young woman, Héloïse.

Hundred Years' War

In the 14th century, local clothmaker Etienne Marcel led a revolt against the Valois regent, forming an alliance with English forces which in the end led to his losing the support of the majority of his followers. He was assassinated shortly afterwards. All through the Hundred Years' War, control of Paris bounced back and forth between English and French forces. When Joan of Arc laid siege to the city in 1429, Parisians sided with the occupy-

ing English and put up stiff resistance. Things finally settled down once Joan of Arc had succeeded in putting Charles VII on the throne.

The period of artistic rebirth that followed under François I continued until a religious crisis provoked the St Bartholomew's Day Massacre, in which thousands of Protestants were killed. However, Henri, king of the southwestern realm of Navarre, escaped and eventually became Henri IV, one of France's most celebrated kings.

Henri is known to have switched his religion from Catholic to Protestant and back at least six times, with apparently no qualms at all. The most memorable occasion was upon his triumphant conquest of Paris. He chose that moment to convert to Catholicism, in order to please the powerful Church fathers of Paris as well as the general population. 'Paris,' he said, 'is well worth a mass.'

Thus began the Bourbon monarchy, France's last. The family lavished plenty of money on the city of Paris, trying to keep the unpredictable citizens, the powerful guilds and the Church content. Louis XIV built hospitals and factories, paved new streets and equipped the city with lanterns. Nonetheless, he preferred to move out to his luxurious palace at Versailles, where he was in less danger than in the gloomy old Louvre, surrounded as it was by narrow alleys crowded with houses right up to the palace walls. That was altogether too close to the common people.

The new court was moved wholesale out to Versailles, where the splendour of the architecture and the rigidity of court etiquette imposed by Louis reduced the nobility to mere courtiers whose most important responsibility

Above: Joan of Arc

might be to hand the king his undershirt at the *Lever du Roi* ('kingrise' as opposed to sunrise). Five hundred cooks prepared Louis' food, and he commanded 4,000 servants.

In the period leading towards the French Revolution, life in Paris took on two distinct forms. On the one hand, wealthy aristocrats and the burgeoning *bourgeoisie* enjoyed sumptuous decadence, carried on intricate social ceremonies and whirled through the restaurants and theatres of Paris. On the bleaker side, most of the population lived in ever-growing misery, while government debts piled higher and higher. While the country's high society was having a fine time, the needs and wishes of the poor were callously swept aside. A bad harvest in 1788 increased the price of bread and revolution fermented as a result.

The destruction of the Bastille prison, on 14 July 1789, swept the past away. Radicals of one hour became the conservatives of the next. Streets were given new names, newborn babies were baptised Egalité, Liberté or République. The First Republic was proclaimed and, in January 1793, King Louis XVI was decapitated in public on the Place de la Concorde.

The storming of the Bastille has long been the symbol of the violent Revolution that shook all of France. As Paris was the centre of revolutionary activities and government, as well as the showcase for the notorious guillotine, the city was unassailably confirmed as the capital of power after the Revolution. 'Paris goes her own way,' wrote Victor Hugo, 'and France, irritated, is forced to follow.' In fact it has been stated several times since that Paris has almost become a mini-state in its own right, a massive urban area in what is essentially a rural country.

Above: Bastille Day, 14 July 1789
Right: Louis XIV, the Sun King

The Making of Modern Paris

Through the First Empire, the Restoration and the Second Republic, Paris continued to consolidate its position as the centre of government, arts, fashion and trade, and was regarded as one of Europe's finest capitals, despite its sordid slums and the fundamentally squalid living conditions of the lower classes.

During the Second Empire (1852–1870), Paris underwent its transformation into the modern city of today. Napoleon III (nephew of Bonaparte) worked with Baron Haussmann, the Prefect of Paris, to carry out extensive urban renewal; thousands of kilometres of new railway track were laid to connect the city with other European capitals; new water mains and a sewerage system were installed to service the two million Parisians now living in the city; great boulevards, avenues and squares were systematically laid out, including the Champs-Elysées, St Michel, St Germain and Etoile, to name a few. These served an aesthetic purpose, but their width also facilitated troop deployment in the event of trouble, and made them difficult for rioters to barricade. Families dispossessed by the construction were often forced to move to the eastern suburbs, home of the belligerent and vengeful National Guard, who felt betrayed by the French government. This influx of the city's poor only added to the area's already notoriously seditious spirit.

The last great struggle between the Parisians and the *bourgeoisie* took place after the fall of the Empire under Napoleon III's Third Republic. Hostile to the notion of Prussian occupation following France's defeat in the Franco-Prussian War of 1870, the citizens withstood a long siege. When the popular National Guard was ordered to disarm in 1871, a revolutionary guard, the *Commune de Paris*, was proclaimed at the

Hôtel de Ville (town hall). From the Montmartre hilltop came the call to arms, as workers and revolutionaries united in the struggle for better representation in government. The bloody repression was carried out not by the Prussians, but by regular French troops: 25,000 *communards* died fighting or were executed, the final 147 being shot in the Père-Lachaise Cemetery. With them went the revolutionary spark that had defied tyrants and kindled republics since 1789.

This bitter and tragic ending is, 130 years on, still a sore spot in the Parisian heart, especially in Montmartre, home to many of the revolutionaries and anarchists at the forefront of the battle. Many of the traditional songs heard in cabarets there still recall the *Commune de Paris*.

Above: Napoleon Bonaparte. **Left:** the Eiffel Tower. **Right:** the liberation, August 1944

Paris in the 20th Century

The period of the late 19th and early 20th centuries is often referred to as *la belle époque*, a time of gaiety and artistic renewal. The Eiffel Tower rose unbelievably high over the city and the Metro tunnelled below. Between 1880 and 1940, Paris was home to more artists, writers and musicians than any other city in the world, both foreign and French, including Picasso, Debussy, Zola, ballet dancer and impresario Diaghilev, and the singer Edith Piaf.

In World War I the city was saved heroically when General Gallieni rushed troops to a counter-offensive in the Marne River valley using all available means. Every taxi in town was requisitioned to carry soldiers to the front.

During World War II Paris was not so lucky, and suffered German occupation for four long and dreary years. The city was not destroyed, however, although charges of dynamite had been placed strategically under monuments. In fact, the German Commander Von Cholitz had orders to blow up the city if the Allies arrived, but he wisely chose to surrender instead. Under General de Gaulle's leadership, the Resistance grew steadily throughout the war, and the troops of the Free French were instrumental in the North African and other campaigns.

Less memorable in retrospect was the role played by the autonomous region of Vichy France, led by World War I general Marshal Pétain. Collaboration with the Nazis was the policy in this region, even though this had harrowing implications for the city's Jewish population in particular. In the end, 25 August 1944 was one of the craziest and happiest days in the city's history, partly because General Eisenhower diplomatically allowed the French troops, under the leadership of General Leclerc, to be the first to enter Paris.

After the rationing, death and horrors of war, Paris prospered in the 1950s and early 60s. Bebop, rock'n'roll and tourists travelled across the Atlantic. But the war and its horrors cast long shadows; post-war thought was dominated by the dark existentialism of Jean-Paul Sartre and Albert Camus. In addition, France lost two major colonial wars, the first in Indochina (1946–54) and the second in Algeria (1954–62).

In 1968, the city suffered a social upheaval. Discontented students staged

a sit-in and riot police were sent in to restore order. Trade unions supported the students and paralysed Paris. De Gaulle, now president, fled the city, just as kings and emperors had done before him, fearful of the wrath of its citizens. He relinquished power to his former prime minister Georges Pompidou.

In 1977, reform made it possible for Parisians to elect a mayor for the first time. Jacques Chirac was the first to enjoy this powerful position. In addition, each *arrondissement* elects its own mayor, and the administration of many city affairs is delegated out to separate town halls. In 1989 France celebrated the bicentennial of the French Revolution, an event that led to an orgy of self-congratulation, and major celebrations in Paris. The Eiffel Tower was also given a complete overhaul for this year.

In 1995 the then Mayor of Paris, Jacques Chirac, was elected as the fifth President of France, ousting François Mitterrand, who had held office for 14 years. Like Napoleon III before him, Mitterrand left behind a legacy of public works in the city: radical improvements at the Louvre Museum, including the glass pyramid by I M Pei enclosing its main entrance, the Opéra at La Bastille, the new Finance Ministry at Bercy, the Grande Arche at La Défense, the La Villette Museum and Science Park, the Arab World Institute opposite the Ile St Louis, the Musée d'Orsay, many extensive new road and tunnel systems to ease traffic, the development of outlying areas, and improved public transport. The result of all these new projects, combined with the 19th-century achievements of Napoleon III and Baron Haussmann, is a striking yet harmonious cityscape.

By 1997, Chirac's tenuous popularity as president had sunk to an historical low, which was borne out in the June elections when socialist Lionel Jospin was made prime minister, creating a second cohabitation with the right.

The undeniable charm of Paris lies in these tensions and juxtapositions – political, artistic, social and architectural. The spirit of the city today is still a mixture of fractious Gaulish rebellion and refined Roman arts, spiced with the exotic contributions of immigrants from Africa and Asia. A mad poet in Montmartre, a brash young businessman at La Défense, a fashion model in diamonds at the Dior boutique, an African student on the Left Bank, an early-rising baker kneading croissants: Paris is home to all. Its streets are living theatres, so walk them and observe.

Above: Tour de Paris

HISTORY HIGHLIGHTS

52BC Lutetia founded by the Romans and occupied by the Parisii.

AD300 Germanic invasions by the Alemanni tribe. The city settles on the Ile de la Cité and takes the name of Paris.

451 Paris repels Attila the Hun with the help of St Geneviève, who becomes the focal point of a cult.

6th century Clovis I brings the Frankish people to settle in Paris.

987 The Capetian dynasty begins, bringing years of prosperity.

12th century Trade booms. The cathedral of Notre Dame is built on the Ile de la Cité. King Philippe Auguste orders the construction of a great wall around the whole city.

13th century The universities of Paris and the Sorbonne are created.

1356–8 Revolt led by clothmaker Etienne Marcel against the Valois dynasty. Marcel was assassinated after making an alliance with the English.

1572 Fervent religious debate leads to the St Bartholomew's Day massacre, in which thousands of Protestants died.

1594 Henri IV takes Paris.

1682 Louis XIV moves into the luxurious Versailles palace and turns the nobility into mere courtiers.

1789 The storming and subsequent capture of the Bastille prison heralds the French Revolution.

1793 Execution of Louis XVI.

1804–48 The First Empire, under Napoleon Bonaparte is declared, and is then followed by the Restoration of the (constitutional) Monarchy.

1848 Revolution in Paris; the Second Republic is declared.

1860 The number of *arrondissements*, or districts, rises from only 12 to 20. Today's smart 16th has its designation changed from the unlucky 13th.

1853–70 During the Second Empire under Napoleon III, nephew of Bonaparte, Baron Haussmann gives Paris its present shape and appearance, particularly notable for its grand boulevards.

1870–1 Paris is under siege by the Prussian Army.

1871 The *Commune de Paris* civil rebellion ends in bloodshed. The rebels are executed by government forces.

1889 The World Fair provokes the construction of several key monuments, most notably the Eiffel Tower.

1890s The Dreyfus affair involving a Jewish army captain who is imprisoned on false spying charges, reveals the anti-Semitism prevalent on the right.

1914 Paris escapes a German invasion, thanks to the military governor, General Gallieni.

1940–4 The German army occupies Paris. Liberation comes on 25 August 1944.

1968 General strike (led by student population) paralyses the city. President de Gaulle, now very unpopular, eventually hands over power to Georges Pompidou.

1974 Death of Pompidou.

1977 Elections for mayor are held for the first time, Jacques Chirac becomes the first incumbent of the Hôtel de Ville.

1981 François Mitterrand, President of the Republic, initiates a major plan for renewing the city including Le Grand Louvre, the Opéra at the Bastille and the Grande Arche of La Défense.

1989 Celebrations in honour of the Bicentennial of the French Revolution, and 100th birthday of the Eiffel Tower.

1995 Mayor of Paris Jacques Chirac is elected president, ousting Mitterrand.

1996 Death of Mitterrand.

1997 Socialist Lionel Jospin is made Prime Minister.

1998 France wins the football World Cup for the first time, defeating Brazil 3-0 in the new Stade de France.

2000 The Pompidou Centre reopens after a two-year renovation.

City Itineraries

1. NOTRE DAME AND THE LEFT BANK *(see map, p22)*

Begin this full day in Paris where the city itself first started, on an island in the middle of the River Seine – the Ile de la Cité. Visit the Gothic cathedral of Notre Dame and then wind your way through the mosaic of streets that make up the Left (south) Bank. Discover the Latin Quarter, a student hang-out since Roman times, with its mix of scholarship and entertainment. Then head to the Luxembourg Gardens, the park most loved by Parisians, and from there to the city's tallest office building, La Tour Montparnasse, in time for sunset.

Start early in the morning and wear your most comfortable footwear. This walking tour takes you from the centre of the city towards its southern end, with plenty of places to stop and rest your feet on the way. So travel at your leisure; you can always hop on the Metro to speed to the next destination, particularly towards the end of the day.

On the **Ile de la Cité** (Metro: Cité), one of two islands in the Seine, site of the earliest primitive city and later the Roman administrative centre, is the main office of the French police and the Court of Justice, all in the grand **Conciergerie**. This imposing chateau stands on the foundations of the city's first royal dwelling. Later it held prisoners during the French Revolution, including Queen Marie Antoinette.

In this pompous setting is a diamond, the **Sainte Chapelle**, with a tall, sharp silhouette that is clearly visible in the overall complex. This narrow and vaulted Gothic chapel (follow the sign inside the main entrance on the Cour du Mai) was built by St Louis, King of France, in 1264. The deep-coloured glass windows set in scalloped stonework and the excellent restoration of the walls and columns lend the building a delicate beauty. Fans of chamber music may wish to note the bulletin board detailing concert schedules. The chapel is open daily 10 am–5pm, except on public holidays, although it is occasionally inaccessible when high-profile trials occupy the courtrooms next door.

Turn back towards Notre Dame via the pedestrian **Place Louis Lépine**, for the flower and bird market. Flower sellers are here Monday to Saturday 9am–7pm; on Sunday, song-birds are the speciality.

Now walk round the corner to the **Parvis de Notre Dame**, a cobbled square in front of

Left: the nave of Notre Dame
Right: a stained glass window, Sainte Chapelle

the great cathedral (open daily 8am–6.45pm; tours available). **Notre Dame**'s stone foundation was laid in 1163 but it was only completed about 200 years later. The scene of various dramatic episodes in French history, from medieval executions to the coronation of an emperor (Napoleon I), the cathedral's ancient walls are steeped in history, reflected in the innumerable faces and figures carved upon them. The three portals (main doorways) to the cathedral are typical examples of Gothic religious art, each a 'book' for the illiterate of the Middle Ages, recounting the stories of the Bible and the lives of various saints. Inside, 29 separate chapels line the nave, transept and choir. The **Rose Windows**, 31ft (9 metres) in diameter, have been extensively restored but parts still date from the 13th century.

The carved wooden choir stalls are early 17th century, and the **Pietà Statue** decorating the large altar at the far end of the cathedral was commissioned by Louis XIII during the same period, an offering in thanks for the birth of his son and heir to the throne, who eventually completed the memorial. In veneration on either side of the fallen Christ and his earthly mother are statues of the regal father and son.

In the **Treasury** (Trésor; closed on Sunday and religious holidays), located off the south aisle to the right of the High Altar, there are displays of religious artefacts, embroidered robes and jewelled chalices. The **Crypt** (open daily 10am–5pm; entrance charge) focuses on Paris's archaeological finds from the Roman period until the 19th century.

As you leave the church, you will see signs to the **Bell Tower**, and if you are up to a 270-ft (82-metre) spiralling ascent, you can visit the huge brass bell and come eye-to-eye with the stone gargoyles who contemplate the city from their privileged perch.

Leave the cathedral, walk around it to the right, go through the little park

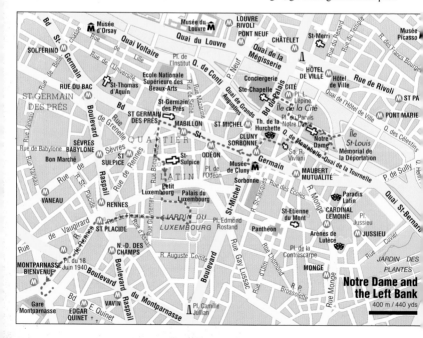

Notre Dame and the Left Bank

400 m / 440 yds

and to the end of the island. There you will find an unusual and starkly moving monument in memory of World War II deportees to German concentration camps (**Mémorial des Martyrs de la Déportation**, open daily; closed noon–2pm) set down into the ground. Descend into the pit through narrow passages between thick, rough walls, and come face to face with black metal bars. There is a feeling of desolation, yet the monument is strangely calm: a windless sun-trap inviting rest and reflection.

From there, take the Pont St Louis to the next island, the placid **Ile St Louis**. The attractions of this 'island of calm' in the storm of the city are the shady riverfront, the fashionable art galleries, cosy, lace-curtained tea rooms (try **La Charlotte de l'Isle** for the ultimate hot chocolate and Wednesday afternoon puppet shows). At 31 Rue St Louis en I'Ile (the other end of the bridge from Ile de la Cité) is **Maison Berthillon**, where you can sample possibly the best ice-cream in Paris while sitting in the sun.

Books and the Latin Quarter

When you're ready, backtrack across Ile de la Cité and cross the Seine to the Left Bank, where a walk along the *quai* affords a fine view of Notre Dame and its flying buttresses, as well as an opportunity to browse among the green bookstalls, which also sell unusual postcards, prints and maps. There are some collector's items to be ferreted out here. More books, new and second-hand, and mostly in English, are in store at the historic **Shakespeare and Co** in Rue de la Bûcherie, just off the left of the tiny Square Viviani. The spirit of famous (and would-be famous) expatriate writers haunts the shop, which is well worth exploring.

Head south into the centre of the **Latin Quarter**, one of the busiest parts of town and favoured by students, shoppers and good-time seekers. These

lanes, filled in the evening with the aromas of Greek and Middle Eastern cooking and busy with entertainers, recall much older times, despite the electric lights and modern fashions. Street performers set up here as they have for centuries, and pass a hat around the crowd. Through the occasional kitchen door left ajar you may see a chef spooning up steaming heaps of Algerian *couscous*. But although this is a popular tourist quarter for good-value dining out, you shouldn't really expect to find the best cuisine in Paris here.

At the minuscule **Théâtre de la Huchette**, the troupe has been playing *The Bald Soprano* for more than 50 years. Tickets are

Above left: a gargoyle on Notre Dame
Right: St Mary's Portal, Notre Dame

available. Amble down the pedestrian streets of La Huchette and La Harpe up to **Boulevard St Michel**. Walk up to the crossroads with **Boulevard St Germain**, where the two big roads meet and thereby set the limits of the famous Latin Quarter.

On the far corner stands the **Musée National du Moyen-Age – Thermes de Cluny** (9.15am–5.45pm, closed Tuesday and public holidays), the only surviving Gothic residence in Paris, next to the ruins of a Roman bath-house. This is one of the best museums in a city that boasts some of the world's finest exhibition spaces. The building lends itself to the display of furnishings, fabrics, architectural ornaments and religious reliquaries from the Middle Ages. Upstairs, the museum's prize is the tapestry series *La Dame à la Licorne* (*The Lady and the Unicorn*), a 15th-century depiction of the five senses plus a sixth, mysterious and unexplained sense that is left to your imagination.

Food and Shopping

After much medieval food for thought, you may be hungry. You will find plenty of choice for lunch up the Boulevard St Germain at the crossroads called **Odéon** (Metro: Odéon). The **Chope d'Alsace**, 4 Carrefour de l'Odéon (tel: 01 43 26 67 76), will satisfy the heartiest appetite with typical food from Eastern France (especially *choucroute* – sauerkraut with pork cuts and sausages),

grilled meat and seafood. The list of daily specials, which is often as long as the regular menu, is based on the chef's mood and the morning's market. Prices are fair and the wine list is tempting.

Thus revived, your next step is to continue up Boulevard St Michel towards **St Germain des Prés**. Along the way, you pass Rue de Buci on the right-hand side and Rue Mabillon on the left, both leading to colourful markets. There are boutiques for every kind of clothes all along the way, from the classic Marcel Fuks for men to the wacky, unisex Atomic City and shops for parents of fashion-conscious children (or vice versa).

The church of **St Germain des Prés** (Metro: St Germain des Prés) is one of

Top: the Musée National du Moyen-Age, Thermes de Cluny
Above: enjoying lunch al fresco in St Germain des Prés. **Right:** the Jardin du Luxembourg

the city's oldest (built in the 11th and 12th centuries, Romanesque in style). The square is also well known for the cafés **Flore** (tel: 01 45 48 55 26) and **Les Deux Magots** and the **Brasserie Lipp** (tel: 01 45 48 53 91), hangouts for the literati since Jean-Paul Sartre and Simone de Beauvoir held court here.

Turn down Rue Bonaparte, away from the church and towards Montparnasse, to find more stylish shops on and around the pleasant **Place St Sulpice** (Metro: St Sulpice). Less animated than St Germain, this square and its 18th-century fountain have a dignified charm. The church, where author Victor Hugo was married, is welcoming despite its monumental proportions; there is a fine old pipe organ inside (check the bulletin board for concerts); the first chapel on the right (Chapelle de Sainte Agnès) was decorated by Eugène Delacroix, one of the greatest painters of the Romantic period. As you leave St Sulpice, look up to the building on the other side of the square and maybe you'll catch a glimpse of France's favourite actress, Catherine Deneuve, leaning out of her window.

Elegant Gardens

As afternoon wends its way to evening, just a short walk down Rue Henry de Jouvenel (immediately left out of the church) and Rue Ferou brings you to the **Jardin du Luxembourg**. Enter by the **Petit Luxembourg Museum**, which has changing exhibitions, and reach the central pond by way of the **Palais du Luxembourg**, once a royal palace and today the seat of the French Senate. If you stroll to the far end of the gardens and look over the top of the palace, you should be able to see Sacré Coeur perched on the Montmartre hilltop, like a fat white pigeon roosting above the city.

Take a break under the shade of the chestnut trees. The Jardin du Luxembourg is much more of a recreation area than the Tuileries, and a particular favourite with many Parisians because of its elegance and central location. But don't linger after dark, or you'll find yourself camping out, as the high gates are locked at nightfall by bell-ringing guardians.

Leave the park by the west exit (level with the round pond) onto **Rue de Fleurus**, where Gertrude Stein and her lifelong companion Alice B Toklas lived and reigned over artistic society and the 'Lost Generation' at No 27. Their coterie included Hemingway, Picasso, Ford Madox Ford, Cézanne, Matisse and other artists in the period from 1907 to Stein's death in 1946.

Continue some way down Fleurus before turning right on Notre Dame des Champs (Metro: St Placide) to reach Rue de Rennes. From there you can walk straight down to Montparnasse (or take the Metro) to arrive at the **Tour Montparnasse** at its southern end.

A Bird's Eye View

To get a superb view over the territory you've covered, take the superfast elevator (9.30am–10.30pm, until 11.30pm in summer; last lift 30 minutes before closing time; admission fee) to the 56th-floor terrace and rooftop of the tower. At this height, the traffic below is seen but not heard, and wide avenues ribboned in green trees stretch away below the rooftops with their charac-

teristic red chimney pots. The glassed-in bar provides information on what you're seeing. But the helicopter pad on the very top (the 59th floor) is more exciting. Open to the wind and seemingly unbounded on the sides, it feels a little dangerous (there is no real danger, in fact) – which may be why there are not usually many people up here. Look due north and you can spot the green sward of the Luxembourg Gardens, and a little further in the distance, the square towers of Notre Dame.

At dusk, the sun sets beyond the Eiffel Tower. On a good clear evening, Montparnasse is the ideal place to watch the natural fireworks at the end of day, and the sparkles of artificial light blooming across the city landscape.

Back on the street, you can head for dinner at one of Hemingway's favourite haunts: **La Closerie des Lilas** (171 Blvd Montparnasse, tel: 01 40 51 34 50) or **La Coupole** (102 on the same street, tel: 01 43 20 14 20). The first is rather special; it has a laid-back atmosphere and a piano bar and is more expensive as well as being some way down the boulevard. (It is here that Hemingway wrote *The Sun Also Rises* (1926), and you can see his plaque on the bar. Other illustrious clients include Lenin, Modigliani and André Breton.) The second is a large and noisy place to dance, eat, see and be seen. Both have varied menus; for a complete meal with wine, count on at least 200 francs per person. They're open late, as are many of the cafés and bars, and there are plenty of taxis to take you back to your hotel.

Above: the view from Montparnasse

2. THE GRAND BOULEVARDS (see map, p28)

Today's itinerary begins with a panoramic view of Paris from the Arc de Triomphe. This is the Paris of the grand and sweeping avenues, created by Baron Haussmann in the mid-19th century. Start by walking down the

Champs Elysées to Place de la Concorde and the Tuileries; side-step the Louvre to the Palais Royal; visit the redeveloped Les Halles; round off with the Pompidou Centre.

The first half of this day is spent walking along the long straight line known as the **Triumphal Way**. A major feature of Paris, it is perhaps no longer the most spectacular attraction, even though it now extends to the new Grande Arche at La Défense. The Champs Elysées is still the most famous section of this route. (A hint for those with tired feet: ride down the avenue in green bus No 73 and save some energy).

A familiar landmark, the grand **Arc de Triomphe** (Metro: Charles de Gaulle-Etoile) straddles a hectic, cobbled traffic circle. Construction began in 1806, but it wasn't completed until 30 years later, all in commemoration of the victories of Napoleon Bonaparte. In 1920, the arch became the site for the **Tomb of the Unknown Soldier**; a flame of remembrance was lit.

Napoleon the Little

It was the 'other' Napoleon (nephew of Bonaparte's, known to some as 'Napoleon the Little') who ordered the city planning that gave the **Place de l'Etoile** ('of the star') its name. With the Prefect of Paris, Baron Haussmann, he created the city's wide boulevards flanked by chestnut trees, including the 12 avenues that radiate from the Arc de Triomphe. Partly motivated by the need to control rebellious crowds (hence the wide, straight thoroughfares), the two of them created an architectural legend and advanced the art of urban planning.

You can take an elevator to the top of the Arc de Triomphe (10am–10.30pm; closes 6pm Sunday and Monday, 6.30pm in summer). The view is still largely the same as it was when Haussmann had finished with the city, and includes the **Bois de Boulogne** forest to the west and, of course, the **Avenue des Champs Elysées** below.

One hundred years ago, this glitzy strip was little more than a bridlepath, suitable for closed carriage rides and intimate suppers in discreet restaurants.

Above: the Arc de Triomphe
Right: La Défense from the Arc de Triomphe

Luxurious private homes later gave way to sumptuous hotels, expensive shops and desirable corporate addresses. Now the avenue sparkles at night – not with the diamonds and bright personalities of its heyday, but with heavy traffic and neon lights.

Cinemas, cafés and fast-food places provide most of the entertainment today; the shops and restaurants are generally overpriced and aimed at tourists; the people walking up and down the avenue are mostly foreigners or teenagers from the suburbs who come in for hamburgers and a film.

Modern Attractions

Despite the fading reputation, it is still fun to stroll down the Champs Elysées and people-watch. The top end is dominated by airline offices and the **Tourist Office**, on the south side. On the same side halfway down is the **Hotel George V** (on the avenue of the same name; Metro: George V), which is beautifully decorated and has a fine restaurant and garden terrace.

The size of the Champs Elysées is emphasised by stores such as the **Hippo Citroën** or the **Pub Renault**, where you can check out the latest car models and the Renault Museum over a thick steak or a beer, and the **Virgin Megastore**, an enormous book and record shop.

At this point the avenue becomes far more attractive in summer, with its serene fountains and shady park, and several interesting theatres. To the right just down Avenue Franklin Roosevelt is the **Rond Point** (**Théâtre Renaud-**

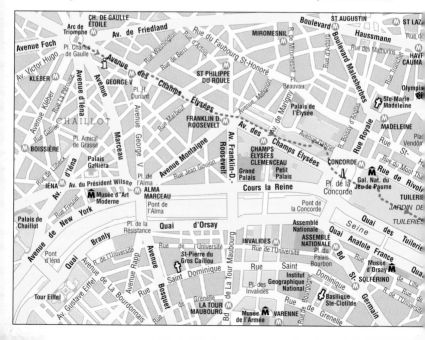

Barrault), which was created by two of France's finest actors. You can walk in for a look at the fun décor, or stop for a drink in the bar. The restaurant **Lasserre** (tel: 01 43 59 53 43) is a little further down this avenue on the right, opposite the Palais de la Découverte. This discreet building is one of the top 10 restaurants in town – for both cuisine and prices. Count on at least €120 per person, but wine from the outstanding cellar may make that substantially higher.

Back in the parkland on the left of the Champs Elysées, the **Espace Pierre Cardin** (half-way to Place de la Concorde) is another prestigious performance space, where a garden restaurant (a favourite with celebrities) features a buffet lunch.

The **Place de la Concorde**, and its commanding obelisk from the tomb of Ramses III in Egypt, is another city landmark. Eighty-five thousand square yards (70,833sq m) of cobblestone, the Place is known for its furious traffic. Try to ignore it and admire the view of the two magnificent palaces on the north side. They are the works of architect Jacques-Ange Gabriel, by order of King Louis XV, and epitomize French Enlightenment style, being at the same time majestic and simple. It was in the Place that Louis XVI was beheaded in January 1793. His last words were: 'May my blood bring happiness to France.'

Garden Respite

Cross the traffic into the **Jardin des Tuileries**, the gardens leading to the Louvre. The central alley is part of the straight line running down from the Arc de Triomphe. Haussmann left his mark here, too, tearing down the remains of a castle and opening up the streets. In the park you'll find outdoor cafés, a children's play area and, finally, almost inside the encircling arms of the Palais du Louvre, the **Arc de Triomphe du Carrousel**, a miniature mirror-image of the Arc de Triomphe itself, which marks the end of the lengthy Triumphal Way.

At this point you could make a detour across the Seine, to the **Musée d'Orsay** *(see page 96)*, the impressive French

Left: Place de la Concorde
Above: a famous name

national museum of 19th-century art (it actually covers work from 1814–1914), housed in an elaborate renovated Beaux Arts railway station.

Back on the northern side of the river, by the Arc du Triomphe du Carrousel, if the Louvre also beckons at this stage, turn to itinerary 10: *The New Louvre (see page 61)*. However, I suggest you postpone your visit, and dive across the busy **Rue de Rivoli**. Walk through the arcades past the gilded statue of Joan of Arc to the Place du Palais Royal (Metro: Palais Royal). The adjacent Place Colette is home to the **Comédie Française**, the national theatre founded by Molière. Follow the arcades to the entrance of the **Palais Royal Gardens**. About 200 years ago, the Palais was a royal palace, until Philippe d'Orléans, who was living there, sank into debt. He added arcades and rented boutique space to solve his cash-flow problem. It became a popular speakers' corner and played a major role in the Revolution.

Today the shops are still there, beyond the square of black and white columns designed by Buren. Most of the shops offer antiques and collectors' items, especially coins and military decorations. These dim little boutiques, which have somehow survived the arrival of the fashion designers' showrooms, are full of rare treasures for those who know how to value them.

Part of the Palais is now occupied by the Ministry of Culture; other apartments are still in private hands. It is said that these apartments are beyond price – families hang on to them forever. It is easy to see why: they are centrally located yet quiet, soothing to the eye and spirit. Sometimes you can glimpse a high-ceilinged room behind a heavy brocade curtain. Among the famous ex-tenants are writer Colette with her numerous cats, poet and director Jean Cocteau, and his favourite actor Jean Marais.

Bibliothèques Old and New

Slip out the far end of the rectangular gardens and cross the tiny Rue des Petits Champs. To your left are **Galerie Vivienne** and **Galerie Colbert**. These restored skylit passages with mosaic floors lead to Rue Vivienne and the old **Bibliothèque Nationale**, not far from the Opéra. You can still visit the exhibition rooms of Coins, Medals and Antiques (Tuesday to Saturday: 1–5pm, Sunday and holidays: noon–6pm, closed Monday). The books, however, are now kept in the controversial new **Bibliothèque François-Mitterrand**, designed by Dominique Perrault in the Tolbiac district. If you want to investigate, go to the Pyramides station on the Avenue de l'Opéra and take the swanky **Meteor Metro** (line 14), which drops you within a few minutes at Bibliothèque François-Mitterrand station. If you are neither a scholar nor an architecture fan, continue down the Rue des Petits Champs.

To your right is the **Place des Victoires**, a delightful circle that was constructed to display the statue of Louis XIV in the centre. Now fashion is king both in the Place and the narrow streets radiating out from it. The designers' boutiques are New Age outposts among the plethora of regal architecture.

Around the corner (past the main post office on the Rue du Louvre) is the restaurant **Au Pied de Cochon** (tel: 01 40 13 77 00), one of the best known in Paris, in a row of restaurants on Rue Coquillière. In a throwback to older times, when market deliveries were made in the wee hours before stalls set up, it is open day and night. One of the favourite dishes of the market hands was the thick, cheesy onion soup, which is still found on the menu. For a complete meal, count on about €50 per person.

From Food to Fashion

You are now on the fringes of **Les Halles**. The name refers to the city food market that clogged up the neighbourhood streets from the 12th century until 1969, when it was demolished in the interests of safety and urban renewal. Now a more ordinary commerce takes place in about 200 boutique within the multi-level shopping centre (Metro: Les Halles).

But don't go down the escalators – unless you really want to go shopping. Instead, have a quick look inside the rather sombre and grand **St Eustache** to your left. Then go along Rue Berger to the lively **Place des Innocents**, where there's usually a good crowd gathered around the fountain. Parisians who knew it before renewal deplore the high-priced boutiques and cafés that have moved in, but it is as animated and attractive as ever.

At the corner of Rue Berger and **Rue St Denis**, take a good look up and down. Rue St Denis marks the city's main red-light area, which becomes more overt several blocks further down to the left. The area in which you stand is fairly tame, and although there are sex shops here, there are lots of cheap eateries and interesting shops too.

Left: Maillol sculpture
Above: inside St Eustache. **Right:** a market stall

All the comings and goings in the pedestrian areas, and the variety of commerce and nightlife here, help Les Halles to retain something of its former dynamism. Drifters, bargain hunters, sensation seekers, local residents and young people all add to the atmosphere, but hang on to your wallet.

Head south from Place des Innocents towards the river and then turn left onto Rue des Lombards. Use it to cross Boulevard Sébastopol into the region of Paris known as the Marais. Instantly you will find yourself in the Marais' characteristic narrow, winding streets with small shops and bars. Turn left up Rue St Martin to **St Merri**, an ornate medieval church nestled tightly between the shops and restaurants. You may hear music floating out of its doors, as there are frequent concerts in the church, particularly at weekends. The church bell has been tolling the hours since 1331 and is the oldest in Paris.

The Pompidou Centre

Now you are just around the corner from the most visited attraction (twice the numbers for the Louvre) in the city. This modern museum, known affectionately as 'Beaubourg' after the street that runs behind it, has been looming on your horizon ever since Les Halles. Its official name is the **Georges Pompidou Arts and Cultural Centre** (open daily except Tuesday: Centre: 11am–10pm, Museum: 11am–9pm; Metro: Rambuteau), and it acts as a massive magnet for this whole area of Paris, drawing people through the narrow streets to its doors to the tune of eight million visitors a year, or 24,000 per day – of whom 60 percent are French. The museum has become so popular that it is hard to remember the passionate debate about its 'inside-out' architecture (blue units are air-conditioning, green ones are water circulation, red tubes are transport routes and yellow ones indicate electric circuits); today it is much loved, and comments of the 'it looks like an oil refinery' variety are rarely heard. Due to its popularity, Beaubourg began to age prematurely: a massive programme of remodelling was needed. Now completed after more than two years of work, the fully renovated centre reopened on 1 January 2000, more impressive and exciting than ever.

Above: Georges Pompidou Arts and Cultural Centre, also known as Beaubourg

While many Parisian museums seem to be staid, whispery places, this one is an exception, even before you enter. Fire-eaters, mime artists, musicians and an assorted crew of urban nomads have adopted the sloping cobbled terrace. Students love the library and music room. The ride is free on the escalators that snake up the outside of the building in a transparent tube to the level 6 rooftop restaurant and viewing platform. By the southern end of the building, between Beaubourg and St Merri church, you can see a colourful fountain, created by sculptors Niki de Saint-Phalle and Jean Tinguely to pay homage to composer Stravinsky's *Firebird*. Its mixture of grotesque creatures and contraptions spouting water is much appreciated by children.

The Pompidou's permanent collection is the **National Museum of Modern Art**, on levels 4 and 5. There is a more serious art-appreciation atmosphere in these well-lit and comfortable rooms. Paintings and sculptures include works from different periods and schools: Fauvism, Cubism, Futurism and various artists including Matisse, Kandinsky, Mondrian and Dubuffet. These permanent exhibitions are well worth the visit: the only equivalents in the world are the Museum of Modern Art (MOMA) in New York and Tate Modern in London. If you find yourself faced by a long queue, it is probably for a temporary show on level 6. Occasionally, these are quite controversial.

In the entrance hall, there is usually a free exhibition, invariably something zany and challenging, such as a show of household lamp design, some 'sonic environments' in which to immerse oneself, or an exhibition of mud and clay architecture. On the mezzanine level is a post office and internet café.

Film, Music and Dance

The **Salle Garance** specialises in films that don't often make it to local theatres. For avant garde sounds, there is the **IRCAM** (Institute of Research and Co-ordination into Acoustics and Music), a prestigious centre created by Pierre Boulez. The museum also welcomes dance and theatre troupes to its basement stage.

There is a complete posting of all the centre's events and exhibits on the ground floor; some things are free. The information booths stock brochures in many languages, and there is a very good bookshop, as well as a design shop selling a selection of works by modern designers.

For dinner this evening, I suggest one of two options. The first, **Restaurant du Palais Royal** (tel: 01 40 20 00 27) at 43 Rue Valois, is a popular dining spot overlooking the Palais Royal gardens. You can expect to pay around 45 euro per person. Or try the rather less chic but just as French 'Smoking Dog', **Au Chien Qui Fume** (tel: 01 42 36 07 42), at the top of Rue du Pont Neuf. You'll find shellfish and hearty French cooking at reasonable prices, as well as all-day service from noon until 2am every day (expect to pay around 30 euro per person).

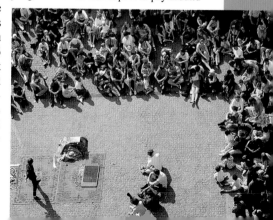

Right: entertainment outside Beaubourg

3. MARAIS AND BASTILLE *(see map below)*

This itinerary takes you through one of the most distinctive and well-loved areas of Paris: the Marais. The beauty of the buildings lining the narrow, twisted streets can be traced to the 16th and 17th centuries, when well-

to-do Parisians built their *hôtels particuliers* (private residences).

You should begin your day at the **Hôtel de Ville** (Metro: Hôtel de Ville). This is the seat of the main branch of local government, and has been the fiefdom of the Mayor of Paris since 1977.

The first Hôtel de Ville was built along the bank of the River Seine during the Renaissance, at the height of the neighbourhood's popularity. It was burned to the ground during the in-surrection of the Commune de Paris in 1871, and Parisian architect Viollet-le-Duc, famous for his restoration and recreation of medieval edifices, undertook its reconstruction.

There is a convenient post office in the Hôtel de Ville (on the side with the very pleasant court-yard), and on the Rue de Rivoli there is an entrance to an exhibition area with some information about the town.

You may be tempted to tarry on **Rue de Rivoli**, a very busy shopping street, but to discover the Marais, you must take quieter paths, and I sug-gest you begin at the **St Gervais Church**, which is located in a square on the other (eastern) side of the Hôtel de Ville. The monumental Gothic style of this church is original, not reconstructed. Restoration has been carried out,

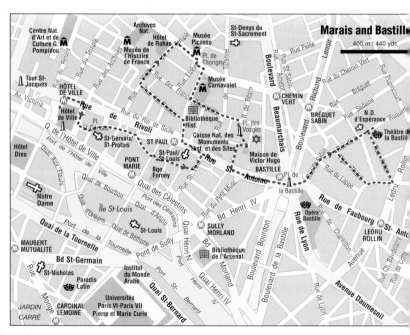

however, most notably after a German shell exploded here in 1918, killing 51 people who were attending a Good Friday mass.

Continue up **Rue François Miron** to the left of the church, contemplating the row of houses from No 4 to 14 built in 1732. Further along, some distance past half-timbered houses on the left, No 68 is another remarkable residence, the **Hôtel de Beauvais**, dating from 1665. Louis XIV gave it to his mistress, and when she was gone, Mozart lived there briefly. Turn right into Rue de Jouy and go across the crossroads by the Tribunal and into Rue Charlemagne. Hidden away to the right (signposted) in this quiet residential district is the **Bibliothèque Forney**, open in the afternoons. Before it became the city's historical and fine arts library, this building was known as the Hôtel de Sens, which the Archbishop of Sens began building in 1470. The pointed towers on the corners are a familiar landmark to Parisians. Later, the mansion was inhabited by Marguerite de Valois, first wife of Henri IV, notorious for her penchant for young lovers.

Continue down the rather dull Rue Charlemagne to where it suddenly becomes far more interesting at **Rue St Paul** (Metro: St Paul). This little street is a favourite of mine, with its exotic boutiques and restaurants. Take it left up to Rue St Antoine. This wide avenue leads back into the Rue de Rivoli, but you should cross it and turn right to reach the **Hôtel de Sully**, which now opens its doors to the public as the **Caisse Nationale des Monuments Historiques**. This umbrella organisation offers the best guided tours of Parisian monuments, museums and sites. Inside, you can visit the lovely courtyard (open for concerts in summer) and the current exhibition, and also pick up an illustrated map of the Marais (weekdays 9am–6pm; Saturday 10am–1.15pm and 2–5pm; closed Sunday and public holidays).

The Jewish Quarter

Retrace your steps down Rue St Antoine past the church, turn right on Rue Malher and go down **Rue des Rosiers**. This is the heart of the Jewish Quarter, as the specialised shops and restaurants tell you. One of the best places to eat is **Jo Goldenberg's** (No 7; tel: 01 48 87 20 16). The Goldenbergs came from Russia and borsch is a favourite starter, and stuffed carp is the star of the menu. Prices are moderate, unless you opt for caviar.

At the end of the street, turn right on Rue Vieille du Temple and follow it some distance to Rue de la Perle. Turn right again to reach the Place Thorigny and the **Picasso Museum** (1 April to 30 September 9.30am –6pm, 1 October to 31 March 9.30am–5.30pm, closed Tuesday), on the left off a little square. The museum occupies the **Hôtel Salé**, so-called because its 17th-century owner grew rich through the lucrative activity of collecting taxes on salt. Oddly, the modern masterpieces fit superbly into the well-restored décor. The chandeliers, benches and chairs were designed by Picasso's friend Alberto Giacometti. The paintings and other works of art were part of the artist's legacy, and are arranged chronologically. There are

Left: St Gervais Church
Right: part of the façade of the Hôtel de Ville

also works by other artists, part of Picasso's private collection. The museum opened in 1985. Despite the long queues, it is worth persevering to see so many of this prolific artist's works in one place.

Continue your walk down Rue du Parc Royal, then right into Rue Payenne and past the two little parks. This part of the Marais has grown more chic since the museum opened, with trendy boutiques and art galleries. Some have set up in butcher's or baker's premises, and kept the original shop-fronts. Several other Renaissance *hôtels* are in the middle of restoration.

Time for a Tea Break

Stop on the corner of Rue des Francs Bourgeois at **Marais Plus**, a wonderful gift shop and tearoom. The shop has a great collection of the most eccentric teapots. Refresh yourself with a big piece of freshly baked cake or pie and a pot of fragrant tea.

Just around the corner a few places to the left, on Rue de Sévigné, is the **Carnavalet Museum** (10am–5.40pm, closed Monday). This is the city's historical museum, again in a well-restored *hôtel*. Rarely crowded, it exhibits aspects of urban life from the Middle Ages through the French Revolution, and also shows some of the furnishings and souvenirs of Mme de Sévigné, a colourful 17th-century character renowned for her wonderful correspondence. The museum itself is a creaky old place with a quiet little garden.

Walk the rest of the way down the

Above: the Picasso Museum. **Left:** Louis XIV as Roman emperor, Carnavalet Museum

boutique-lined Rue des Francs Bourgeois to the **Place des Vosges**, a highlight of the Marais, and a unique Parisian square. The red brick arcades give it a singular appeal. This is the oldest square in Paris, and its name is in honour of the first French department to pay its taxes to the new Republic.

At the far corner of the square, **Victor Hugo's House** is open to the public at No 6 (Tuesday to Saturday 10am–5.40pm, closed Monday and national holidays). The author of *Les Misérables* was also an expert carpenter: some of the furniture on display was crafted by his own hands. The covered arcades of the Place des Vosges are animated much as they must have been in Hugo's time, with street singers and accordion players adding to the atmosphere. Restaurants, tea rooms, fashion boutiques and some interesting shops line the square; you'll find places selling antiques alongside others full of modern items of interior décor for the home. One of the prettiest restaurants is **La Guirlande de Julie**.

Revolutionary Honour

Leave the Marais down Rue de Birague and Rue St Antoine and turn left for the **Place de la Bastille** (Metro: Bastille). In the centre of the former site of the notorious prison captured on 14 July 1789 stands the **July Column**. It was erected in the 19th century to honour victims of the revolutions of 1830 and 1848. Caught in mid-flight at the top is a golden statue, the *Génie de la Bastille*, a representation of Liberty. The old Bastille prison has long gone. In its stead a new fortress has taken shape, all silver and glass, look-

ing sleek and impenetrable. This is the **Opéra de la Bastille**, one of President Mitterrand's great projects. Plagued by controversy from the start, the Opéra is now up and running. Time will tell if it achieves its goal of making great music more accessible to the population of Paris.

Your destination now is **Rue de la Roquette**, branching off near the Opéra and heading east all the way to the Père Lachaise cemetery. You are now out of both the winding Marais and the grand and uniform Haussmann's Paris, and away from the tourists. This street becomes increasingly run-down as you head out of town. Once the site of a women's prison where public executions were spectator sports, the street has shed its grisly reputation and is now a trendy place. If you are ready for dinner, you will find plenty of choice here. There are several Japanese restaurants, and other ethnic styles of cooking are represented.

If eating can wait, just wander along the street, which offers an eclectic mix of shops, including a model train shop, some small fashion boutiques and some shops specialising in artefacts for the home – they have some very quirky items that might make unusual souvenirs. The secondhand

bove: merchandise at a shop in the Place des Vosges

bookshop next to the **Théâtre de la Bastille** has a good collection of postcards – not just the usual shots of the Eiffel Tower.

Retrace a few steps, then turn down **Rue Keller**, where you can visit several small galleries displaying a variety of mainly very modern works. Continue to the end of the street and turn right onto Rue de Charonne, where **Lavignes Bastille** is one of the best-known galleries in the neighbourhood. Andy Warhol has exhibited here. The homemade cakes in the window of the **Café Charonne** next door may tempt you in. When refreshed, carry on to the last street on our

agenda, the Rue de Lappe, on the right off Charonne. There are more galleries here, with exhibitions that change regularly, so it is impossible to predict exactly what you will find. Prices may be negotiable.

Rue de Lappe is a good place to stop for dinner and enjoy the buzzing nightlife and atmosphere of this lively area. There is a variety of eateries here, offering the cuisine of different countries, including Spanish tapas bars. One option worth trying is **La Galoche**, at the beginning of the street. The restaurant's name derives from the word for 'shoe' used in the region of Auvergne. La Galoche serves typical hearty fare from the region in a warm friendly atmosphere (expect to pay around 200 francs per person). You can even buy a pair of wooden shoes here, if you feel inspired by the rustic ambience.

Such shoes, however, would not be appropriate footwear for a night of dancing at the **Balajo** (tel: 01 47 00 07 87), three-quarters of the way down Rue de Lappe. This fun club is both authentic and inexpensive, with Art Deco flourishes and a big dance floor. The Balajo is just one of several nightspots you will find along this street.

Dine in Style

If your day has left you feeling a little tired, you will be glad to know that you are almost back at the Place de la Bastille, and can head for the **Brasserie Bofinger** (3 Rue de la Bastille, just off to the west side of the Place, tel: 01 42 72 87 82), although it's probably best to reserve a table. Settle back and enjoy its comfortable, old-fashioned ambience, brass, mirrors, leather and ceramics. The food is worthy of the oldest brasserie in town. For around 200–250 francs per person, you can enjoy a real feast; the menu features fresh seafood, *choucroute*, and traditional French dishes and wine.

Above: in the spirit of Bastille Day

4. BOIS TO EIFFEL: WESTERN PARIS *(see map, p40)*

Today's itinerary features a part of Paris known by its district number – the 16th – and largely ignored by tourists. It is a luxurious residential area bordering on the spacious western park of Paris, the Bois de Boulogne. Down by the riverside, the district puts on a much more familiar face at Trocadéro, where the monumental and museum-laden Palais de Chaillot opens its two wings to frame the city's most famous landmark: the Eiffel Tower. This is a long itinerary; you can shorten the walk by starting at the Musée Marmottan, missing the Bois altogether.

On a map, the **Bois de Boulogne** is a large green rectangle bordered on the western side by a bend in the River Seine and on the eastern side by the 16th district of Paris. The main road-entrance to the 2,000-acre (872 ha) park is at **Porte Dauphine** (Metro: Porte Dauphine). Start early and walk along the Route de Suresnes, or venture off the roadway on to the footpaths leading to the **Lac Inférieur**, a long and narrow artificial lake.

You will share your stroll with many Parisians from joggers to rowers on the lake. In some parts of the Bois, prostitution is practised openly by 'hitchhikers' standing near the roadway. By day this is less common.

You may see people waiting for the horses to start running at the **Auteuil Race Track**, studying their racing forms and the sports pages of the daily newspapers. Rose lovers should walk deeper into the park along the Route aux Lacs and the Route de Bagatelle to the **Bagatelle Gardens**. This fragrant park is a favourite spot for romance. The expression *faire la bagatelle* is a quaint euphemism for 'making love'.

Child's Play

Children should head northward to the **Jardin d'Acclimatation** (Metro: Porte Maillot or Sablons). For a small entrance fee, you can visit the collection of farm animals and climb, roll, swing, slide, run, crawl and jump on a great range of playthings. For the price of tokens purchased inside, you can board the miniature train, visit a children's museum, and go on carrousel or mini-motorbike rides. The garden has an old-fashioned atmosphere, reinforced by the people who frequent it: wealthy white-gloved grandmothers from the 16th *arrondissement* with children dressed by the top designers.

When you are ready to leave the Bois, amble down the footpath known as the Allée aux Dames which leads away from the Lac Inférieur. This heads over the traffic to the **Fortifications**, named after an archaeological site revealing the last remains of the old city wall. Walk out by the Route des Lacs where it leads to the Place de la Porte de Passy. Cut straight across the wide Boulevard Suchet and veer left on Avenue Ingrès into the pleasant **Jardins de Ranelagh** (Metro: Ranelagh).

Above: freewheeling in the Bois de Boulogne

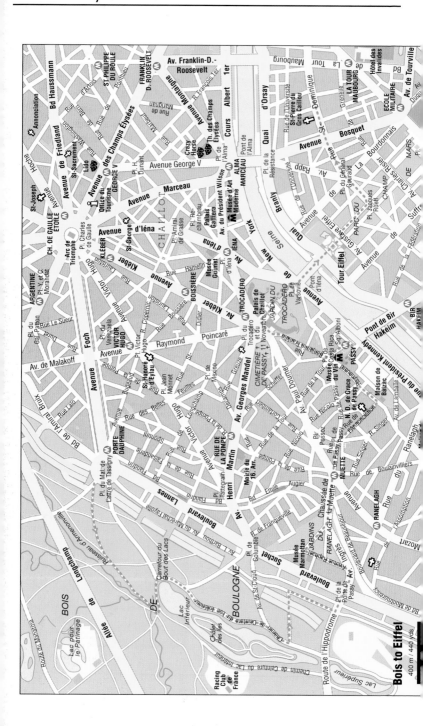

Top right: the dragon ride at the Jardin d'Acclimatation
Right: Balzac's home

The trees here seem to form a vaulting ceiling, green and airy, above the soft sandy floor, transforming the little park into a veritable cathedral. This is where the **Musée Marmottan** (10am–5pm, closed Monday) sits discreetly on a corner at 2 Rue Louis Boilly on the northern side of the park. The museum is devoted to the work of Impressionist painter Claude Monet. Delicious and colourful as summer itself, the collection includes some 100 Monets in addition to paintings by Gauguin, Sisley and Renoir. Downstairs you will discover Monet's renowned *Water Lilies*, giant canvases painted in his garden in Giverny. Also on display is the Marmottan family's collection of furniture and medieval manuscripts. Strangely enough, the different types of art seem quite at home together in this beautiful old building.

Exclusive District

Walk out of the triangular-shaped park by its tip on Chaussée de la Muette and straight ahead through one of the busiest intersections of the 16th, **La Muette** (Metro: La Muette). There is a revealing story about this wealthy, rather snobbish part of town: when first incorporated into the city, the area was designated district number 13. Well-to-do residents didn't appreciate the unlucky number, and used their collective political clout to have it changed. The very buildings evoke privilege, with their massive wooden doors, decorative carved façades – the architect's name is often engraved by the doorway – and manicured flower beds. You'll see au pair girls with small children, and maids going shopping with Madame's list in hand.

Around **Place de Passy**, shopping is busier than ever in the covered market. Here elegant ladies eye ribs of beef and squeeze avocados as they plan their dinner parties for the evening ahead. Teenagers turned out in the latest fashions stop in chic little bakeries. Take the pedestrian street that leads off the little square (Passy), the Rue de l'Annonciation, which is lined with a variety of

interesting market stalls. Follow it down to the Rue Raynouard (Metro: Passy). At the end of the street, past Notre Dame de Grace de Passy, turn right. You will see **Maison de Balzac** (10am–5.40pm, closed Monday and public holidays) on your left, lending a bit of high-spirited irreverence to this posh neighbourhood. The prolific writer lived here from 1840 to 1847, while revising the 90 volumes of his novel series *La Comédie Humaine*. Downstairs, the complex genealogy of the series' 2,000-odd characters has been mapped out, and Balzac's corrections can be seen in the margins of original manuscripts. One look at his cramped writing and the extensive annotations and you understand why typesetters charged double to do his books.

Balzac liked to work from two in the morning until five in the afternoon. He kept going all this time by drinking copious quantities of black coffee which he concocted himself, which explains the prominent coffee pot. An-

other feature of the house is its secret exit onto a back street: this was his way of escaping from unwelcome callers – particularly debt collectors.

Wine and Water

Return on the Rue Raynouard through the apartment blocks to the tiny Passage des Eaux, on the right, which descends steeply to Charles Dickens Square. The **Musée du Vin** (10am–6pm, with its own restaurant) is located here. This simple little museum is very aptly situated, for the cellar cuts into the riverbank hillside that once belonged to the monks of Passy, who made their own wine and stored it there 400 years ago. In the 17th century, the street was crowded with people coming to drink the mineral water flowing from the ground, reputed to have curative powers. It became a fashionable spot for lovers to meet, and Napoleon was seen here frequently.

During the French Revolution, the last monks were chased from the abbey and the convent was destroyed. None of the other buildings survived after 1906. The cellars were mostly forgotten until the 1960s, when the owner of the Eiffel Tower Restaurant started storing his wine there. The present museum opened its doors in 1984. The exhibits comprise a hotchpotch of tools, containers and wax figures, and the walls are covered with engravings and drawings relating to wine. The boutique has a selection of vintage wines for sale, as well as all sorts of corkscrews, serving baskets, glasses, decanters and racks. And if it is all too much to resist, you can wind up with a little wine-tasting right on the spot.

It is a short walk (or one stop on the Metro from Passy) from the wine museum to the **Place du Trocadéro** at the end of Boulevard Delessert. Follow the garden path up to the **Palais de Chaillot** on the hilltop. In the centre of the park, steps and ramps are alive with fountains and youngsters on rollerblades and skateboards. The outdoor restaurant on the left is called the

Above: sculpture on the Palais de Chaillot

Totem (tel: 01 47 27 28 29), reached by taking the entrance to the Musée de l'Homme. The view over the gardens and across the river to the Eiffel Tower is enough to draw you in. The food is also a cut above the usual museum cafeteria offerings, and reasonably priced at about 180 francs per person.

The flat terrace between the two wings of Chaillot, lined with golden statuettes, is usually busy with African merchants selling bracelets, leather goods and toys. The curved buildings and monumental landscaping date from the World Fair of 1937, and today the complex is a formidable bastion of culture. It would be impossible to visit all of the exhibition space in one day, but the following museums deserve a mention. All are closed on Tuesday.

Cultural Adventure

The **Musée de l'Homme** (Wednesday to Monday, 9.45am–5.15pm) is devoted to anthropology. Eskimos, mummies, primitive man, mysterious civilisations all have a place here. The **Salon de Musique** has a collection of musical instruments through the ages.

The **Musée des Monuments Français** (Wednesday to Monday 10am–6pm) occupying the northern wing of the Palais is another favourite, especially among the French. Roman, Gothic and Renaissance architecture from all over the country is represented here. It offers a fascinating journey through the French countryside at different points in history. Also on the hilltop is the **National Popular Theatre** (or Théâtre de Chaillot), which is so large it makes you feel as though you've walked into the belly of a whale. The main house seats an audience of 1,150 people; classical works are usually performed here. The foyer and the smaller house (Gémier) offer more offbeat programmes. Finally, the **Musée de la Marine** (Wednesday to Monday 10am–5.50pm), a maritime museum, contains plenty of material designed to appeal to children of all ages.

As you cross the Seine, up looms the **Eiffel Tower**. The 985-ft (300-m) tower, once vilified, now reigns as the queen of Parisian monuments. A face-lift in time for its 100th

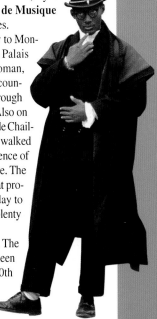

Above: the Place du Trocadéro
Right: street entertainment, Paris-style

birthday in 1989 coincided with the expiration of a private lease. The beauty treatment removed tons of rust and a sagging restaurant. New lights paint the metal lattice-work silver and gold at night.

The glass-walled lift jerks up at an alarming angle. The machinery is unique; a special team of employees does nothing but oversee spare parts, which must be made individually. If you are prepared to go up on foot you can rest on the landings and read about the people who have used the tower for daring exploits, such as riding down on a motorbike.

On the first level, an exhibit and short film recount the story of Gustave Eiffel, the tower's architect, and the 1889 World Fair for which it was built. The tower was meant to be temporary, and no one ever intended that it should become the symbol for Paris; in fact in 1909, a proposal was made for its dismantlement. But it was the advent of radio transmission and the need to site an aerial which gave the tower, the world's highest structure when first built, a reason to stay.

On the top platform is **The Jules Verne** restaurant (which has a private elevator for patrons only). To dine here, you need to make your booking well in advance (tel: 01 45 55 61 44). It specialises in fine *cuisine traditionnelle* and its prices are among the highest in Paris, though you are paying as much for the view and the experience as the food.

The tower is open daily until 11pm; until midnight in July and August. Tickets are a different price for each level. Be prepared to queue for tickets and again for the lifts. The long park stretching away from the riverside and under the tower's splayed feet is the **Parc du Champs de Mars** (Metro: Bir-Hakeim or Ecole Militaire), once a military drill field. At the far end is the 18th-century **Ecole Militaire**, home of France's officer-training academy and several academic institutions.

A Perfect Ending

Walk some distance down the colourful and varied **Rue St Dominique**, which you will find about half-way down the park on the left. At No 79, stop in at **Thoumieux** (tel: 01 47 05 49 75). This restaurant is another Parisian landmark (Metro: Invalides). Open daily, its speciality is *cassoulet*, a hearty dish based on white beans and duck which is superb when cooked well, as it is here. Thoumieux's ambience is just as appealing as the food – informal and relatively inexpensive. Alternatively, you may decide to take a boat ride along the Seine to Notre Dame (boats depart from the quay just below the tower), and join up with the tour *Notre Dame and the Left Bank* described in Itinerary 1 (*see page 22*).

Above: the most famous landmark in Paris – the Eiffel Tower

5. FROM RODIN TO DIOR *(see map, p46)*

The 7th and 8th districts of Paris, separated by the Seine, are elegant neighbourhoods. The morning starts amongst the sublime forms in the Rodin Museum, then moves north via Les Invalides to the river. Afterwards visit the Grand and Petit Palais, then on to Avenue Montaigne for some *haute couture*.

The **Rodin Museum** (Tuesday to Sunday 9.30am–5.45pm, winter until 4.45pm, closed Monday) is at 77 Rue de Varenne (Metro: Varenne). In the morning, the rose garden and its still pools are shadowed by the **Hôtel de Biron**, built in 1728 as a private residence. August Rodin lived and worked there more than 100 years later, and bequeathed it to the State on the condition that his works be exhibited in the house and park. Though he is now recognised as one of the greatest sculptors of all time, with a technique comparable to that of Michelangelo, Rodin was a figure of controversy in his own lifetime. Early exhibitions of his work brought cries of fraud from 'experts' who claimed that his human figures were so anatomically precise they could only have been made using real bodies to form moulds for casting. In this setting, the timeless figures do seem to live and breathe.

Monumental Sculptures

You enter under the gaze of what is probably Rodin's most famous statue, *The Thinker*, set up high amongst the greenery. To the left, *The Burghers of Calais* re-enact the noble gesture that saved their town from the ravages of the English army in the 14th century. Against the wall, *The Gates of Hell* is a monumental work wreathed with shapes of demons and the damned.

Inside the house, the wooden floors, marble staircase, gilt mirrors and French windows embrace large works, including the prominently displayed *Adam and Eve*, as well as small ones, such as *The Kiss*, a delicate study in white marble. There are works by other artists, including Camille Claudel, Rodin's assistant and mistress. The difficulties of the creative life were multiplied for her as a woman, and she eventually lost her mind and was all but forgotten in a mental institution. The film *Camille Claudel*, starring Isabelle Adjani and Gérard Depardieu, created renewed interest in the artist and her relationship with the master. Go out the back door and you can wander under the grape arbour and rest on a bench.

When you leave the *hôtel*, turn left onto Boulevard des Invalides and walk to **Place Vauban**. Here the Avenue de Breteuil stretches out like a green carpet, and you can view the giant complex known as **Les Invalides**.

The first building that stands out is the golden-domed **Eglise du Dôme**,

Right: inside the Rodin Museum

completely regilded in the city's bicentennial facelift in 1989. Therein lies the **Tomb of Napoleon I**, six layers of coffins beneath a sarcophagus of dark red stone. Bonaparte's remains are kept company by a number of great generals and his son, the ill-fated 'King of Rome'. The decoration inside the church is distinctly military: flags captured from enemies of the Empire hang on the walls.

The other vast wings of the Invalides were initially built as a veterans' home, but today's old soldiers make do with more ordinary housing, while the buildings house the **Army Museum** (daily 10am–5pm, until 6pm in summer; closed some public holidays) and administrative offices. The museum is the largest of its kind in the world and exhibits everything from cannons and suits of armour to taxi cabs mobilised for the Marne offensive in World War I. In summer, a nightly sound and light show conjures up the glory days: check the announcements for times and languages.

Napoleonic images of grandeur are projected beyond the main entrance across the windswept **Esplanade des Invalides**. On both sides the streets lead away to numerous government ministries and official residences. The *ensemble* culminates in the **Pont Alexandre III**, perhaps Paris's most splendid bridge (Metro: Invalides). Built in 1900, the bridge spans the Seine with a single metal arc. The golden statues and distinctive lamp-posts are typically Parisian.

Crossing the river, you arrive in the middle of the **Grand Palais** (10am–8pm, closed Tuesday) and the **Petit Palais**, museums with per-

Above: the majestic Petit Palais

manent and changing exhibits (10am–5.40pm, closed on Monday). Look at the big posters outside to find out what's on. Occasional blockbuster shows attract massive crowds that form into a long queue all the way around the park. These typical Art Nouveau wrought-iron and glass 'crystal palaces' were built for the Universal Exhibition of 1900. The gardens that surround them are pleasant and shady; take a breather here and watch the world pass by (Metro: Franklin D Roosevelt or Champs Elysées Clemenceau).

Designer Shopping

You'll need your breath for exclamations on the last leg of this itinerary: the main branch of 'The Golden Triangle' of shopping streets: **Avenue Montaigne**. Here you can gaze at the displays for Chanel, Cartier, Dior, Vuitton, Nina Ricci, Ungaro, Valentino… and more than your combined credit cards could imagine. Even if you don't venture into the boutiques, you can get an eyeful just strolling down the street, which is kept spotlessly clean and often decorated in holiday style by the wealthy tenants.

This brings you back to the riverbank at **Alma Marceau** (Metro: Pont d'Alma), where you can stop in a café or brasserie for lunch, or head for a **Bateaux Mouches** tour boat just underneath the bridge. You can pick up a snack as you wait for the departure, and spend a pleasant hour off your feet, gliding through the city. Boats leave every 20 minutes or so in summer; at night batteries of lights illuminate the riverside architecture. Don't bother trying to listen to the static and crackle of the multilingual, taped commentary, just sit back and look.

6. PÈRE LACHAISE *(see map, p48)*

This suggestion for a peaceful morning in eastern Paris takes you to a resting place for the famous, and a Parisian village.

Those who know it love to return, and some who go there never leave – such as Frédéric Chopin, Molière, Rossini, and more recent luminaries including Edith Piaf, Gertrude Stein, Oscar Wilde, Jim Morrison and Yves Montand. The place, of course, is the **Père Lachaise cemetery**, in eastern Paris, the city's largest and loveliest burial ground (Metro: Père Lachaise). At the main entrance on Boulevard de Menilmontant, visitors can pick up a map pinpointing the more famous graves, and the small bookstore also sells a surprising variety of guides to the cemetery. Indeed, most of the people wandering about seem more curious than bereaved.

At first glance, this older part of the cemetery near the entrance appears to make use of above-ground burial, but look more closely and you will see that the tiny houses in this city of the dead are actually small chapels, often in a state of disrepair. Walk up Avenue Principale and turn right to find the monument marking the grave of Héloïse and Abélard. She was a student of the controversial theologian in the 12th century, and secretly became his wife. Her father's fury separated them; Abélard ended up castrated in a

Right: a sculpture of Chopin on his tomb

monastery, and Héloïse in a convent, but they left their letters to posterity, professing a pure and faithful love.

Make your way along the shady paths to the chapel on the hilltop for a view over the stalwart chestnut trees, spreading like guardian spirits over the myriad monuments. You may see the benches occupied by old women feeding the numerous cats who make their homes amongst the monuments. Others come to visit the grave of the spiritualist Allan Kardec, and leave odd mementos or practise bizarre rites in front of his tomb.

Rebel Heroes

Of historic interest is the **Mur des Fédérés**, located at the back of the cemetery in its eastern corner where grotesque and striking war memorials spring from the earth. The wall was where the last of the anarchist rebels of the *Commune de Paris,* a courageous uprising against Prussian domination in 1871, were lined up and shot. The bullet holes are still visible. Also in this top corner is the **Jardin du Souvenir**, with many monuments commemorating the dead of World War II, including some dedicated to the victims of Auschwitz, Buchenwald and others. There are also monuments to different members of the French Resistance. If you are especially interested in this period, you may be lucky and come across war veterans or historians here.

Leave the quiet behind slowly, exiting at this corner down the steps onto **Rue de la Réunion** (named after the Indian Ocean island which remains a French territory to this day), a street more full of baby strollers than cars. This is the sort of neighbourhood where people close up the shop and go home for lunch, a *baguette* under one arm, and then have an afternoon snooze.

Keep going across Rue de Bagnolet to **Place de la Réunion**, which looks as if it has been picked up and transported from a much smaller town in France – or even directly from the tropics, as the local African

Above: onlookers at Jim Morrison's grave

[Map: Père Lachaise — 400 m / 440 yds. Labels include N.D. de la Croix, PELLEPORT, Tenon, GAMBETTA, Place Martin Nodaud, Pl. Gambetta, Rue Belgrand, PORTE DE BAGNOLET, PÈRE LACHAISE, Columbarium, CIMETIÈRE DU PÈRE LACHAISE, Mur des Fédérés, St-Germain de Charonne, St-Cyrille St-Méthode, Square H. Karcher, PHILIPPE AUGUSTE, ALEXANDRE DUMAS, Boulevard, Bon Pasteur, St-Jean Bosco, Pl. de la Réunion, Orteaux, Rue d'Avron, Bd de Ménilmontant, Av. Philippe Auguste, Rue de Bagnolet, Boulevard Mortier]

community adds a colourful dimension to the tiny circle. It may be rather ramshackle and not particularly elegant, but this is just as much the true Paris as the world famous downtown boulevards.

Continue through this neighbourhood of small shops and furniture craftsmen down the Rue des Orteaux and just under the old train line into Rue du Clos. This takes you to **Le Village St Blaise**, tucked discreetly into this eastern end of Paris (Metro: Porte de Montreuil). Part of the neighbourhood is a modern public housing development and shopping centre with a purple colour scheme. The quality and originality of the architecture and planning belie the 'moderate rent' nature of the housing.

Exotic Cuisine

Turn left and walk up Rue St Blaise. Up here is a good find for lunch, an Algerian restaurant called **Le Village de Paris** (24 Rue St Blaise, tel: 01 43 56 66 63). Couscous, the main item on the menu, has become very popular in Paris, and not only among the large North African population. This family restaurant is warm and homely. Big dishes are brought out to the table for you to garnish your plate as you choose with a selection of exotic appetisers. Then follows the couscous: four varieties of fluffy semolina, a bowl of piping hot vegetables and sauce; a little tub of hot pepper sauce for spice; and either mutton, chicken or beef.

After the meal, pass around the plate of fresh dates. If you like North African food, head directly here, you can't find better, and you can't beat the prices (150 francs gets you any dish). The street also has a number of other possibilities, including a dainty tea room for delicate eaters (**Le Damier**).

Watching over Rue St Blaise, its single rose window like a benevolent eye, is **St Germain de Charonne**, whose country-church character suits the neighbourhood well. This church has become so popular for weddings that Parisians sign up a year in advance for the pleasure of saying *oui* at the altar. Walk up the steps on its left side, and take a look at the cemetery – which makes quite a contrast to Père Lachaise.

From here the Rue des Prairies and Rue des Pyrénées will take you back to **Place Gambetta**, the heart of the 20th *arrondissement*, and the Metro.

Above: Rue St Blaise

7. SHOPPING TOUR *(see map, p51)*

Looking for a special gift? Ready to brave the fashion boutiques? Then follow this trail. If you're a window shopper only, the route can easily be completed in a morning, but if you intend to go on a spree, it could take the whole day.

There's one Metro station in Paris that everyone seems to pass through regularly, and it bears the name of the famous building above it, the **Opéra**. It's a lively neighbourhood, the hub of the Grands Boulevards, and a business centre to banks, travel companies, and the nearby Stock Exchange (La Bourse).

If you need to replenish your wallet before your spree, stop off first at **American Express**, on Rue Scribe, which has many services for travellers including banking and foreign exchange. Or if you're in a hurry and have cash, try the automatic money exchange machine at the BNP **Bank** right on the Place de l'Opéra. Twenty-four hours a day, you can slip your own currency in the slot and get Francs in return, or use your ATM or credit card. Various travel and ticket agents for tours and shows are around here, so it's a good opportunity to line something up for the evening or another day.

Crowning Glory

Start your tour proper at the **Palais Garnier** (open 10am–5pm) as the Opéra building is officially known. This 'wedding cake' was completed in 1875, the crowning achievement of the plan designed by Haussmann to open up the centre of Paris. You can walk into the vaulting foyer for a glimpse of the eclectic décor, and on days when no rehearsal is in progress, you can go into the theatre itself. A splendid surprise awaits you overhead: painter **Marc Chagall's ceiling**, a frolicsome work in blue and pearl tones, in striking contrast to the sombre red and gold opulence of the hall. Guided tours of the Opéra (in French) are conducted at 10.45am Monday to Saturday.

Just across the street is the **Grand Hotel**, and its sidewalk café, the **Café**

de la Paix, one of the ...
Paris. The expansiv...
café, taking up a who...
de l'Opéra, is no...
you're in a hurry, but, as ...
gests, a venue for a moment of peace m...
the midst of the crowd.

Revived and refreshed, head for *les Grands Magasins*. These department stores sprang up in Paris during the 19th century and have been popular among Parisians and visitors ever since. On Blvd Haussmann you'll find the **Galeries Lafayette**, famed for its sparkling interior. Orient yourself by heading for the central escalators and the store directory in French and English, plus a bilingual hostess who can help you find that perfect gift. Other services at the store include a fashion consultant and duty free forms for recovering sales taxes at the airport. Fashion is the biggest seller here, whether it's off-the-rack designer or the Galeries' own label. Beautifully made accessories like stockings, scarves and headwear can suddenly seem like essential items of clothing. The lingerie department is legendary.

Home from Home

Across the street is a branch of **Marks and Spencer**, the British chain store, which seems just as popular as its French cousins – even among visiting British for some reason. And another block down is **Printemps**, which advertises itself as 'the most Parisian department store'. It certainly is the most beautiful inside: the domed ceiling built in 1923 is now a historic monument. The perfume department is supposed to have the largest selection of lotions in Paris. There are make-up demonstrations and fashion shows almost every day, and the same services for English-speaking tourists as in the Galeries Lafayette.

Head next for the pedestrian **Rue de Caumartin** (Metro: Havre-Caumartin). There is more room to breathe on this street, bordered by smaller shops and the 18th-century **St Louis d'Antin church**. Free

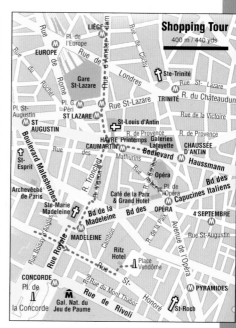

Left: inside Galeries Lafayette
Above: Parisian elegance on display

organ concerts are regularly scheduled on weekends; leaflets inside the main entrance give the dates. More spontaneous street music concerts are likely to be in progress at any time.

But if you're not ready to interrupt your shopping, continue your tour back down Rue Tronchet and Rue Vignon, which lead from St Lazare to the Place de la Madeleine. **Rue Vignon** in particular is worth a meander. It has smaller boutiques that may not carry the big designer names found on the Avenue Montaigne but are nonetheless filled with interesting ideas and prices. For unusual little gifts or souvenirs, I can recommend **La Maison du Miel** (24 Rue Vignon), offering French honey in pretty little pots and other beautifully packaged products.

The monumental church in the centre of **Place de la Madeleine** (Metro: La Madeleine) is not very welcoming. More rewarding are the window displays at **Fauchon**, which confirm France's reputed supremacy in the art of presenting food. You can eat here *sur le pouce* (informally), a favourite lunchtime option among people who work in the neighbourhood: just point at whichever delicacy you fancy and a member of staff will pile a portion onto a plate and you can eat it (standing up) at the counter.

Garden Feast

If you would rather sit with a picnic than eat on your feet, head for the nearby Tuileries after a stop at one of the other exotic food shops on the

Place de la Madeleine. Try **Hédiard**, where you can fill your basket with caviar, tropical fruits and a vintage wine. The staff will wrap your purchases in chic black and red paper and tie them up with ribbon.

Rue du Faubourg St Honoré and **Rue St Honoré** continue the chic shopping. These streets are the traditional (if somewhat outmoded) address for major designers like **Hermès** and **Gucci**. Just around the corner is the **Place Vendôme**, elegantly symmetrical and home to the Ritz Hotel and **Cartier** jewellers, whose major outlet is nearby on Rue de la Paix.

If you've still got money left at the end of your day, why not enjoy tea at the **Ritz** (proper attire is required), owned by the Egyptian proprietor of London's Harrods, Mohammed Al Fayed, and engraved on many people's memory as the hotel from which the Princess of Wales set out on that fatal car journey in 1997. If you feel you deserve something a little stronger than tea, you can adjourn to the hotel's **Hemingway Bar**, named after the writer who made it his hang-out.

Top: a statue in the Tuileries
Above: evidence of style and wealth outside the Ritz. **Right:** Sacré Coeur Basilica

8. MONTMARTRE AND PIGALLE *(see map, p54)*

Montmartre, perched on a steep hill on the northern rim of Paris, is a legend in itself. It seems to have its own history apart from the city below, its own famous citizens, and its own traditions in entertainment and art. The Sacré Coeur Basilica, a landmark that can be observed from all over the city, is the central tourist site, but not really the heart of its neighbourhood. Be warned: free maps don't show the narrow streets of this itinerary and take a deep breath – visiting Montmartre has much in common with mountaineering.

Montmartre is almost always crowded with tourists. But, surprisingly, a walk of a few blocks away from the central Place du Tertre brings you to quiet streets where stairs tumble down to the city below, quiet as the cats prowling about. If stairs and hills are too much for you, take the Montmartrobus, a special bus line that runs between Pigalle and the hilltop. For the cost of one Metro ticket for a one-way trip, it is the best tour deal in town. Much the same route is also covered by a miniature train (Le Petit Train de Montmartre), which is cute, but no great improvement and more expensive.

Start the itinerary at **Place d'Anvers** (Metro: Anvers). Follow the signs to the *Funiculaire* that lead you up the Rue de Steinkerque. The street is lined with fabric and clothes shops. If you have an eye for that sort of thing, there are nice bits of velvet ribbon, fancy buttons and trims. You can also find the lacy curtains that are so typically Parisian, with unusual designs.

Art for Everyone

At the top of the street, with Montmartre's white basilica rising above you, turn right to walk down to the **Marché St Pierre**. This 19th-century covered marketplace has recently changed its vocation. It is now home to the **Primitive Art Museum** (Musée d'Art Naïf Max Fourny; every day 10am–6pm, except some public holidays), which presents works by artists from around the world, painting in the colourful, magical style that Rousseau made famous. It also runs children's workshops, and the bookshop has an original selection of books,

cards and ideas for activities for children. Look out for postcards that you can cut out into earrings.

Above the Place St Pierre looms the **Sacré Coeur** ('sacred heart') **Basilica**, which was built a mere century ago – small potatoes in this city. Its construction came close on the heels of the *Commune de Paris* uprising against Prussian domination in 1871. The uprising took its inspiration and strength from Montmartre and its anarchist population, who resisted to the last. It was French regular troops who betrayed the *communards*, executing 25,000 of them in the final weeks of battle.

The church was built in appeasement for the bloodshed, and so has never been well-loved by local residents, known as *Montmartrois*. To this day, it is often mocked in cabaret songs on the hilltop (locally known as *La Butte*).

Amazing View

Climb the switchback stairway, or relax in the **Funicular railway** (use one Metro ticket) to reach the terrace in front of Sacré Coeur. From here you have a splendid view over the city, and coin-operated telescopes to help you pick out your favourite places. Look south to the centre of Paris, and you should distinguish the brightly-coloured Pompidou Centre and the two square towers of Notre Dame, which stand out from the otherwise low-rise and uniform city centre. This vista is on the opposite side of Paris from the panorama seen at the top of the Montparnasse Tower (*Itinerary 1; see page 26*). The Eiffel Tower is off to the right, black and solitary on the skyline.

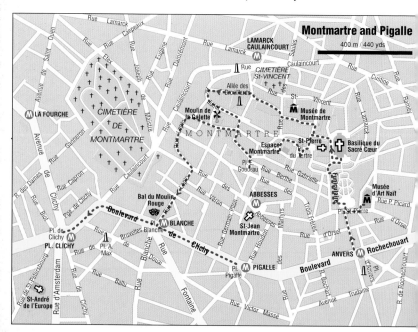

Montmartre and Pigalle

If it is a warm day and you're feeling hungry after your ascent, take the steps to your left until you come to **L'Eté en Pente Douce** (tel: 01 42 64 02 67), a tiny restaurant on Rue Muller, overlooking the Sacré-Cœur gardens.

Now walk around to the right behind the church. It is like going behind a curtain and discovering a magical theatre set. Follow the lane round to the left and the **Place du Tertre** greets you with strings of bright lights and swirls of colourful people. You will return to the square later. Battling through the crowds towards the *point de vue* on the corner of Rue Poulbot you will find the new Espace Montmartre (10am–6.30pm), home to over 300 works by **Salvador Dalí**, and its popular shop.

Stroll down Rue du Mont Cenis, leaving the crowd behind, and take a left on Rue Cortot. No 6 was the house Eric Satie lived in while composing his delightful piano pieces. The painter Utrillo, who captured so many of *La Butte's* houses and cafés in his work, also lived on this street, with his mother, artist Suzanne Valadon.

Community Spirit

At No 12 Rue Cortot is the **Musée de Montmartre** (11am–6pm, closed Monday) situated in an 18th-century manor house along with the **Montmartre Cultural Centre**. Its windows overlook the **Montmartre Vineyards** and Rue St Vincent. Every October, there is a big harvest celebration here. Obviously, given the size of the vineyard, there is not a lot of wine bottled, and its value is more sentimental than gustatory. But it is a great source of pride to the *Montmartrois*, proving that they still have a strong community spirit. On the lower floors of the museum, you can see the recreated study of composer and violinist Gustave Charpentier, and a reconstruction of Utrillo's favourite café, l'Abreuvoir. The graceful garden setting and the care with which original objects have been preserved and presented make this the best museum to visit in Montmartre.

Go to the end of Rue Cortot and turn right onto Rue des Saules. The vineyards are visible from down here for those who didn't go into the museum, with the Montmartre cemetery behind its wall diagonally across from the vines. A bit further down is **Le Lapin Agile** (22 Rue des Saules, Metro: Lamarck-Caulaincourt), an old-fashioned cabaret which opens at 9pm, and whose last show ends at 2am. The entrance price gets you a spot on a long wooden bench by a scarred table, and a little glass of cherries in *eau de vie*. All night long, guests are treated to 'songs, humour and poetry', in the tradition established here by Aristide Bruant, who was immortalised by the Toulouse-Lautrec portrait showing him in his perpetual black hat and cape.

Left: one of the many artists to be found on the Place du Tertre
Above: Le Petit Train de Montmartre

Many of the roving performers sing songs he composed as they make the rounds of cabarets on *La Butte*. Le Lapin sounds quaint, but it is also fast-paced, and you'd have to have good knowledge of French to appreciate it.

Back up the hill, the restaurant **La Maison Rose** on the corner was the subject of the painting that brought fame to Utrillo. Left at the Maison Rose leads to an elegant corner called the **Allée des Brouillards**. Ivy-covered gates stand before snug houses. The **Château des Brouillards** (Castle of the Mists) stands opposite, in a small park. The house was built in 1772 by an actor from the Comédie Française, and several artists lived there after him. Now boarded up, it is a spooky place, haunted by the souls of poets.

Renoir's Windmill

Go down the steps of Rue Girardon to Avenue Junot. Follow the curving avenue back up to Girardon and Rue Lepic; at the crossroads stands the **Moulin de la Galette**. The windmill was made into a dance hall in the 19th century, and celebrated in a painting by Renoir. Vincent Van Gogh lived with his brother in a pretty little house at No 54 Rue Lepic.

Cross Lepic into an alley called Rue d'Orchampt, and follow it round. At the end is a row of artists' studios that look much like the **Bateau Lavoir** did when Picasso and Braque painted there. The site of their Montmartre studios is around the corner on **Place Emile Goudeau** (Metro: Abbesses).

Of course, many of the famous artists who lived and loved in Montmartre – Picasso, Apollinaire, Matisse, Toulouse-Lautrec, Marie Laurencin, to name only a few – were also great *bons vivants*. A good time is still on the agenda, and to make the most of your night out, I have three suggestions.

Back in Place du Tertre, try **A La Mère Catherine** (tel: 01 46 06 32 69). The décor is dignified and warm, the menu simple and inviting. The years haven't changed much about this place; it's not unusual to see three generations sitting at the same table. (Expect to pay about 200 francs per person.)

Another more informal option is **Tartempion** (tel: 01 46 06 10 40), on Rue

Above: Place du Tertre is a popular place for artists to sell their work

du Mont Cenis, serving plain fare and tasty desserts at moderate prices (100 francs). On a warm night you can sit outdoors on the terrace.

After dinner, I suggest you stay on La Butte and head for **La Bohème du Tertre** (tel: 01 46 06 51 69). You can't miss this brightly lit cabaret on a corner of Place du Tertre. Head for the back room where musicians play traditional dance music (polka, waltz, and a charleston or two). The crowd really gets going with French drinking songs and old favourites about Montmartre. Order a bottle of wine and dance and sing until 2am.

Feathers and Skin at the Moulin Rouge

Alternatively, there are famous and racier venues nearby. Come down off the hilltop and out of the shadow of the church to head for the naughtier regions of lower Montmartre and Pigalle. Take the twisty Rue Lepic all the way to Place Blanche (Metro: Blanche), where you will find the unmistakable **Moulin Rouge**. Skip the dinner show here, the food is dull and the prices high, but take a look at the photos for fun, and buy a ticket for later if you're interested. The Moulin has been showing feathers and skin for 100 years now, so must be doing something right. Spare a thought to the French poet Jacques Prévert, who used to live just next door, and continue on down the sexy Boulevard de Clichy to the **Place de Clichy** (Metro: Place de Clichy) and the restaurant

Charlot Roi des Coquillages (tel: 01 53 20 48 00). The speciality here is seafood, and what could be better than a plate of oysters or a bowl of bouillabaisse. Count on around 300 francs for a meal with wine.

Also on Place de Clichy is **Wepler** (tel: 01 45 22 53 24), an oyster bar and restaurant favoured by author Henry Miller when he sowed his wild oats in this part of town. Open until 1am, Wepler is in a similar price range to Charlot.

After dinner, you can backtrack to Place Blanche and continue all the way to **Pigalle** (Metro: Pigalle), popularly known to allied soldiers in World War II as 'Pig Alley'. Along the way, there are plenty of strip shows with hawkers to lure you inside. The entrance fee is next to nothing, but the drinks served inside are obligatory and tend to be extremely expensive. For a good high-spirited drag show, try **Michou**'s *Folies Folles* (80 Rue des Martyrs, tel: 01 46 06 16 04): larger-than-life incarnations range from the French torch singer Barbara to Josephine Baker and Shirley Bassey, and they can be seen and heard by everyone.

Pigalle is changing all the time; **Folies Pigalle**, for example, has gone from sex show to alternative theatre to music hall. Nightclubs offer a different brand of entertainment and attract a new crowd. **La Locomotive** (90 Blvd de Clichy) goes full steam ahead until 5.30am. It is a lot bigger than the Folies, has two separate discos, two bars, a video room and live music. And when the club closes, you can go back up the hill for sunrise.

Above: advertisements from the past in a souvenir shop window in Montmartre

9. BY CANAL TO LA VILLETTE *(see pull-out map)*

The canals of Paris? Yes, indeed, and although there are no singing gondoliers, there are locks and barges, and a very particular urban landscape. What used to be a trade lifeline has now been restored for leisure use. Discover this surprising waterway and the modern museum complex that has been built along its banks, Parc de la Villette. This is a good itinerary for kids, particularly if they're tired of walking.

Redevelopment of the area around La Bastille began with the improvement of the **Arsenal Marina** (Metro: Bastille). The marina was once a very active commercial shipping port; adjacent to the Seine, it joins the **Canal St Martin** leading eastward out of the city. At Bastille, the canal goes underground, emerging again beyond Place de la République. Board the **Canauxrama Tour Boat** (tel: 01 42 39 15 00) at Arsenal Marina, opposite No 50 Blvd de la Bastille, for a three-hour journey eastward. Departures are at 9.45am and 2.30pm daily and the commentary is in French only.

Going Underground

Napoleon built the canal partly to get more water into the city centre and thus earn the citizens' affection; in those days average daily consumption was one litre (just over two pints) per person, as opposed to 200 litres today. As you glide under the city, the canal is lit by sidewalk gratings sending eerie shafts of light down to the water. The different colours of mortar indicate where restoration work has been carried out; the area directly overhead has been untouched since the canal was built. At Quai de Valmy and Quai de Jemmapes, you emerge in trees and gardens and yet another unique Parisian landscape. If you wait patiently at the locks you can see how the moss on the canal walls often hides fresh water mussels. On the left bank, your guide will point out the **Hôtel du Nord**, and play part of the soundtrack to the eponymous French movie. When the hotel was recently slated for demolition, neighbours and cinephiles protested so strongly that the famous facade was saved.

Near the **Bassin de la Villette**, warehouses and cafés cater mainly to the leisure boaters on the canal. Some of the industrial space here has been

reclaimed by artists' cooperatives as studio space and undoubtedly this neighbourhood is in for further big changes. Just beyond the port, the canal divides into the Canal St Denis and the Canal de l'Ourcq, two working waterways.

This is the end of your boat ride. What you see all around you now is known as the **Parc de la Villette** (Metro: Porte de Pantin). It is a big cultural complex created in 1986 on the site of the city's former cattle market. The market building itself, a fine example of 19th-century iron architecture to the right of the canal, is now an exhibition space, **La Grande Halle**. Exhibits range from the prestigious and often controversial Paris Biennale contemporary art show to the International Architectural Fair, and even presentations of fashion collections. There is a small space called **La Maison de la Villette** with a permanent exhibit on the history of La Villette.

City of Science

On the left of the canal, the **Géode**, a polished steel sphere that plays weird music, looks like something from outer space that just landed in a pond. Inside, the hemispheric theatre has one of the world's largest projection screens and dizzily slanted seating. Movies are made specially for these huge screens. Outside, photographers try to capture its mystery on film.

Reflected in the shiny steel is the **Cité des Sciences et de l'industrie** (Tuesday to Sunday 10am–6pm, Sunday 10am–7pm, closed Monday). It takes

hours to see the whole thing, and the entrance fees for its various sections – waived if you have a museums pass – are quite high. Even if you don't visit the whole thing, you can walk in the main hall for free and look at the exhibits on the ground floor. Brochures and cassette guides are available in English. One of the best parts is a big room for children (of all ages) where visitors participate in experiments using mirrors, electricity and tricks of perspective. There is also a jet pack simulator for armchair astronauts. Other exhibits in the museum cover the universe, the origins of life, the underwater world, plant life, and there are even animal robots in a cybernetic zoo. At every turn hands-on computer terminals inform and amuse.

Short films are shown in different areas, and the ultra-modern **Planetarium** runs several programmes a day (there is an extra charge; get your tickets as soon as you arrive – they go fast).

Next to the northern bridge is a big, grey, square and solid-looking tent. This is the **Zénith Concert Hall**, which can seat up to 6,300 people. It has excellent acoustics and modern facilities, and is often booked for concerts. Opposite, a new wave circus performs under the big top of **Espace Chapiteaux**.

The Parc de la Villette itself is a wonderful place to explore, especially with children. Every Sunday, from 1 March to 31 October, a two-hour guided tour is organised in both French and English (3pm in front of the **Folie**

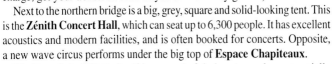

Left: Arsenal Marina has been redeveloped for leisure use
Right: Parisians love their dogs

Information Villette, Metro: Porte de Pantin, free for children under 12).

This urban park – the largest in Paris – spreads over more than 86 acres. Landscape architect Bernard Tschumi designed it, giving each of its 11 gardens a different theme. Kids will enjoy the **Dragon's Garden**, the **Garden of the Winds**, where even babies are welcome to play, and, most of all, the **Garden of Childhood Frights**, with its fairy-tale mystery, dark colours and exciting sound system. Adults will possibly prefer the subtlety of the **Garden of Shadows** and the beauty of the **Garden of Bamboos**.

At regular intervals in the park, you'll find a bright red enamelled steel build-

ing – the contemporary version of an 18th-century French architectural fantasy, known as a *folie*. Each of the 25 *folies* is different and devoted to a special activity. For example, the **Folie Argonaute** leads you to a real submarine that arrived via the Canal de l'Ourcq.

In summer the **Triangle Meadow** is a nice place to sit with your family and enjoy a picnic. You can even watch an outdoor movie, the inflatable giant screen being surrounded by city lights. The park is open, guarded and lit up 24 hours a day.

La Villette's not the place for *haute cuisine*, but there is a selection of cafés in the Cité des Sciences and throughout the park. You'll find a restaurant famous for the quality of its meat in front of the entrance: **Au Cochon d'Or** (192 Av Jean-Jaurès).

The Road Home

To get back into town from here, you can take the Metro from Porte de la Villette. Alternatively, a pleasant route is to take bus No 75, which goes right back to the Pompidou Centre and the Hôtel de Ville. Pick it up at the **Place de la Porte de Pantin**, which you reach by turning left at the road entrance to the Grande Halle and walking up to the big roundabout. However, in common with most Parisian buses, it only runs until about 8.30pm. The bus route takes you past the hilly park of the **Buttes Chaumont**, built in an old quarry and planted in the English Romantic style with trees, islands, and a little Greek temple just peeping through the trees.

After this, the route passes the **Place du Colonel Fabien**, and the headquarters of the French Communist Party, designed by Brazilian architect Oscar Niemeyer. It goes back down to Place de la République and from there turns into the Marais district past the Pompidou Centre and on to the Hôtel de Ville. A short trip down busy Rue de Rivoli and the bus driver takes a break at the **Pont Neuf Bridge**; the name means 'New Bridge', but in fact it is the oldest surviving bridge in town. From the riverbank, note the hundreds of faces carved along the side, each one unique. In 1985, the American artist Christo wrapped up the entire structure in brown paper.

Above: passing time in the park

10. THE NEW LOUVRE *(see pull-out map)*

You may be startled to see references to the 'New Louvre' or 'Le Grand Louvre'. What happened to the old Louvre? The answer is: a lot. Some astonishing changes have been made, not without a certain amount of controversy but definitely with great success. The world's largest museum is still labyrinthine, but it's a joy to discover for old hands as well as for first-timers. And only the French would be so bold as to restructure completely such a major museum.

Le Grand Louvre (9am–6pm Thursday to Monday; closed Tuesday; 9am–9.45pm Wednesday; the Richelieu Wing is open until 9.45 on Monday) is the name ex-President François Mitterrand gave his vast restructuring project. The first, much-delayed, step involved prying the Finance Ministry out of its privileged premises into one wing of the palace. The second major step was to commission the Chinese-American architect IM Pei to create a new entrance and orientation centre.

His design is already world-famous, and although not to everyone's taste it will certainly become part of the architectural legend of Paris. The large glass **Pyramid** rises in the middle of the **Cour Napoléon**. Around it are three smaller pyramids. The area between them is accented by flat, triangular basins in dark stone, raised slightly above the level of the ground. Fountains in these pools complete the composition.

The 'landscape', as Pei calls it, in the tradition of landscape artist Le Nôtre, was designed to bring light into the museum entrance below. It also succeeds in lightening the whole courtyard and the stone façades surrounding it. Thoughtful use of materials and colours allows the sky and water to become elements

Above: inside the Louvre pyramid
Right: a 4,000-year-old scribe

in illusionistic space. The glass is held in place by stainless steel nodes and cables. The result is light and sparkling, a balance of reflection and transparency weighed against the thick stone facade of the old palace, which is heavy with centuries of history. This is the **main entrance** to the museum, but you may be able to dodge any queues by using the Richelieu Passage, off Rue de Rivoli and the Place du Palais Royal. Go through the revolving door and turn down the spiral staircase. The central pillar is an ingenious elevator. This is the **Hall Napoléon** reception area. The museum is not overbearing and has plenty of space.

The new museum services located here are excellent. Ticket windows, the information desk, a bookshop, the rest rooms, and the cafeteria are all easy to find – already a big improvement over the old Louvre. A sit-down restaurant and a sandwich bar provide alternatives for hungry visitors. A wall of screens lists the day's exhibits and activities, and rooms which may be temporarily closed. You will also find a post office, money changing facilities, a cloak room and even an infirmary on this level. The bookshop sells not only postcards and prints, but 15,000 books and periodicals in many languages, with a good selection for children. Casts of art works, jewellery and other gift items are also on sale. English cassette tours are available, and a six-minute film presentation on some of the major works can be seen in the reception. You can take a tour with a guide.

Illustrious Past

When construction began on the new Louvre, major archaeological research was carried out. The fruits of these efforts are now on display in an underground exhibition area called the **Medieval Louvre**. Drawings and scale models show the Louvre at different stages of its career, and reveal how many transformations it had known prior to today. Walk around the ancient walls and most of the medieval fortress, past the towers that were once the gates to the city. The architectural prowess used to display the old foundations so effectively is breathtaking.

There is an exhibition of some of the artifacts uncovered, including many ceramic pieces. The most splendid find was certainly the **Helmet of Charles VI**, found in barely recognisable bits and artfully reproduced. It is on display in the **Salle St Louis**, perhaps the most impressive part of the newly opened area.

Above: Mona Lisa. **Left:** Venus de Milo
Right: the Louvre's foundations

city itineraries

The Louvre, with its new openings and additions, is now bigger than ever, and it is impossible not to get lost. No matter which way you turn in the museum, you always seem to end up in the Egyptian Antiquities. However, like Alice in Wonderland, visitors need only wander at random to discover many marvels. The Pyramid, visible from many different angles through tall windows, and the free handbook from the foyer, will help keep you orientated. On the ground floor, the **Oriental, Egyptian, Greek** and **Roman Antiquities** were the first items to be displayed. Many were brought back from Napoleon's campaigns; when he lost at Waterloo in 1815, many of the stolen masterpieces were reclaimed by their rightful owners. The Egyptian section has, of course, mummies and cult objects, busts and statues of ancient rulers. This famous collection enables scholars to trace the whole development of Egyptian civilisation from prehistory to the Christian era.

Two very famous ladies grace the Greek and Roman rooms: *Venus de Milo* and *Winged Victory*. Their celebrity has somewhat overshadowed the rest of the exhibits. Vast and quiet, the proportions of the rooms are well suited to the pieces. Although the outstanding part of this section is made up of sculpture, there are also bronzes, decorative and useful objects, tools, jewellery and bas-reliefs.

Paintings through the Ages

The second major section of the Louvre collection is dedicated to **paintings**. The collection spans all the European schools, from the 13th to the 17th centuries, displayed on the upper floors. Two-thirds of the paintings are French, and include works by 17th- and 18th-century artists, such as De La Tour, Poussin, Watteau and Fragonard; all can be seen in the **Grande Galerie**. This section's most famous resident is, of course, the Florentine noblewoman *Mona Lisa* (*La Joconde* in French), in the company of an impressive gathering of other works by Leonardo da Vinci. Look out also for masterpieces by Raphael, Titian, and Caravaggio.

Other crowd stoppers here include some of the big paintings in the **Pavillon Denon**: *Napoleon Crowning Josephine* (David), *The Great Odalisque* (Ingres),

The Raft of the Medusa (Géricault), and the revolutionary and inspiring *Liberty Leading the People* (Delacroix).

The third section of the Louvre is known as **Objets d'Art** (Richelieu and Sully wings) and is devoted to furniture, jewellery and small statuary, much of which was confiscated from members of the French royal family at the time of the Revolution. **Apollo's Gallery** (Galerie d'Apollon) is a particularly beautiful room topped by an intricate ceiling painted by Eugène Delacroix. Below, glass cabinets contain the remaining pieces of the Crown Jewels of France. You can see the reputed Crown of St Louis displayed alongside the headgear worn by Napoleon at his coronation. Numerous gem-encrusted and golden objects glitter beneath the guard's watchful eye. Less dazzling – but equally admirable in their own way – is the superb collection of tapestries, furniture and clocks.

Continuing Project

The great redistribution of paintings in the Louvre will take several years to complete. Eventually, paintings will be rearranged in a more chronological perspective, and according to national schools. Already works which were previously not hung for lack of space are on public view, such as *The History of Alexander* by Le Brun, a series of huge paintings that have been rolled up for almost 30 years. Other works of art will be shown on a rotating basis as the process of redistribution is carried out. So even Louvre veterans should be prepared for some surprises.

city itineraries

11. La Défense *(see pull-out map)*

Spend an afternoon in the avant-garde business district on the west side of the city centre. La Défense epitomises French commitment to grand and futuristic projects.

Take the RER line A to La Défense, where the station exits emerge into **Les Quatre Temps** commercial centre. Head for daylight, following signs to the **Grande Arche**. This latter building, at the top of the long flight of steps, is very simplistic in its architecture. Climb the steps, then stop and turn after the last step to witness one of the most magnificent – and oldest – pieces of city planning in the world stretching below you. The Grande Arche is at the end of an axis that runs straight as a die to the Arc de Triomphe, continues down the Champs-Elysées through Place de la Concorde and ends at the Arc de Triomphe du Carrousel, just in front of the Louvre. This axis hasn't stopped growing: there are plans to extend it further west. Turning around again, go into the open centre of the Grande Arche; from here it is worth taking a lift to the top (10am–7pm daily), as the views are quite spectacular.

You may notice that the Grande Arche is slightly at an angle to the axis. This is not a creative spin by Danish architect Johan Otto von Spreckelsen, but thanks to problems in siting the foundations.

Power Base

Most of the buildings of La Défense are headquarters: about three-quarters of the top 20 French companies have their main offices here, as do a dozen or so of the top 50 companies in the world. And even though La Défense was officially completed in 1988 after 20 years' work, many of the original buildings are now being replaced with more advanced constructions.

On a fine day La Défense is a pleasant place to be. Wander down from the Grande Arche and look at the sculptures; there are over 70 signed pieces – including works by Miró, César and Calder. On a wet day the open area can become a deserted canyon of architecture; you could do worse than scurry

into the **Dôme IMAX**, a hemispherical cinema showing pictures ten times the size of those in a normal cinema; or you could view the **Automobile Museum**'s display of the history of the car, exhibiting vehicles from pre-history to 1972. The museum is entertaining, even for those who thought they had no interest in cars. There is also a programme of arts; consult the local press for details.

Top Left: the Galerie d'Apollon, the Louvre
Left: an Egyptian relief
Right: the Grande Arche at La Défense

excursions

Excursions

The region immediately surrounding the city of Paris is called the *Ile de France*, and is rich in history and culture. Some of the most popular spots are also the most accessible, and typical French countryside is never far away. The following destinations can easily be visited in a day. If you leave Paris before noon, you can be back in time for dinner.

1. VERSAILLES *(see pull-out map)*

Versailles comes top on the list of what tourists want to see outside of the city. Rapid transit RER line C, with stops along the left bank of the Seine, will take you there in a jiffy. When you exit at the Versailles station, signs clearly indicate how to walk or take a bus to the chateau, which is only a short distance away.

The inside of the palace is open Tuesday to Sunday 2 May to 30 September 9am–6.30pm, 1 October to 30 April 9am–5.30pm; closed Monday. The vast gardens are open from early morning to nightfall. A guided tour of the palace – unaccompanied visits are not allowed – takes about an hour, but you may have to wait in line almost as long.

It took 50 years to complete Louis XIV's plans for this sumptuous palace, a building that gives new meaning to the word 'grandeur'. In fact, this display of wealth on the king's part foreshadowed the French Revolution. Because he hated Paris and the unpredictable Parisians, and was jealous of the luxurious castle at Vaux-le-Vicomte built by his finance minister, the young Louis planned his opulent *château* well west of the city. He changed the landscape to create his gardens, and installed an elaborate system of pumps to bring water from the Seine to his fountains. More than 1,000 members of court lived in the attic rooms, and life here was as far removed from life outside the palace walls as they could make it. Such daily events as 'the King's Rise' took on momentous importance for the coterie.

Although revolutionary outrage emptied the castle of most of its furnishings, it has slowly been restored; pieces donated by foreign countries or collected and purchased in France have helped to fill out the rooms in a style approaching the original splendour.

In the precise centre of the palace lie the **Royal Apartments**. The staircase linking the king's sitting room to the queen's was added by Louis XV and his mistress, Madame de Pompadour. Look for the secret passage later used by Louis XVI's wife, Marie Antoinette,

Left: formal Versailles in bloom
Right: one of many statues in the palace grounds

to escape the rabble barging through the gates. That escape is the supposed occasion of her infamous reply to the people's cry for bread: 'Let them eat cake' (*Qu'ils mangent de la brioche*). Historians cast doubt on whether she used those precise words, but certainly the sentiment is clear. Poverty and suffering were beyond her imagination, just as the opulence she took for granted is beyond our own.

The **Hall of Mirrors** was used as a royal reception and ballroom. More recently, the Treaty of Versailles was signed here after the end of World War I. Another historic event, which the French are less wont to recall, took place in the hall in 1871: the proclamation of the German Empire. The pint-size **Opera House**, which was built for Louis XV, is a sumptuous hall which once again welcomes special performances, thanks to recent restoration.

Luxuriant Gardens

Outdoors, the park was designed by André Le Nôtre. Three more residences dot the landscape. The **Grand Trianon** (open from 10am; closed lunchtime in winter), on the bank of the Grand Canal, was built by Louis XIV, who sought peace within its pink marble walls. The **Petit Trianon** (open from 10am; closed lunchtime in winter) was built by his successor, but mainly enjoyed by Louis XVI. Marie Antoinette preferred **Le Hameau**, a make-believe hamlet, where she played milkmaid with fine porcelain milk pails.

In the form of a *fleur-de-lys* (symbol of royalty), the **Grand Canal** stretches out from the foot of the terrace, dividing the wooded park in two. The two large fountains in the central alley are the **Latona** and **Apollo** fountains. The first is a weird amphibian allegory dominating the *tapis vert*, the central lawn. The second represents the god driving a chariot led by powerful horses.

Both sides of the park are studded with groves, ponds, exotic bushes, ancient trees and velvety smooth grass. The fountains are so numerous that even a king's coffers couldn't keep them going nowadays, but on the first and third Sundays of June through September, all gush again, their musical splashing joining birdsong. Occasional evening festivities come complete with fireworks and multi-coloured lights.

Above: the grand façade of Versailles

2. CHARTRES (see pull-out map)

Mostly visited for its Gothic cathedral, Chartres is a pleasant and relaxing place to explore. A world away from the big-city mentality of Paris, Chartres is just 97 km (60 miles) to the southwest, an hour's train ride from Montparnasse station.

The medieval town of Chartres sits upon a plateau hemmed in by wheat fields on the banks of the river Eure. The spires of the **cathedral** rise high above the rich plain, welcoming pilgrims since the 13th century.

The cathedral is a near-perfect example of Gothic architecture, but perhaps its most famous features are the **Rose Windows**. Their fame is due to both their beauty and their age, for they date from the 12th and 13th centuries and are among the oldest examples of this type of religious art to be found in the world. They survived a disastrous fire in 1149, in which most of the previous Romanesque cathedral was destroyed, and the French Revolution. During both world wars they were removed and put into safe keeping.

The 'Chartres blue' in the glass is a rich, deep tone that is not found elsewhere. Some panes seem lighter in colour than others, due to an experimental restoration. Light passing through the glass colours the floor, joining traces of the ancient marble **Labyrinth** in the nave. The Labyrinth is symbolic of Christian pilgrimages of the early Middle Ages.

Ancient Remains

Visit the Crypt, the largest and one of the most beautiful in France, to see the site of an even more ancient ritual. The cathedral was built on the grounds of a former Druidic worshipping place. You can see a wall of ancient paintings dating from Gallo-Roman times (4th century). Guided tours of the crypt start from the Maison des Clercs, opposite the south side of the cathedral.

As you leave the cathedral, look up at the two Romanesque towers. The left tower, though known as the 'New Tower', is actually the older, but the delicate Gothic spire atop was added later, in the 16th century. The thicker spire on the right tower is from the Romanesque period.

Behind the cathedral is the former Bishop's Palace, now the **Musée des Beaux Arts**, housing a collection of tapestries, enamels and paintings from the Renaissance to the 18th century. There is also a room devoted to the history of the town. Below the terraced garden behind the museum runs the river Eure. It travels past the **Eglise Saint André**, a deconsecrated Romanesque church used for concerts. Follow the path along the river, past the wash houses and the remains of the old city wall, to the **Place St Pierre**, where another set of magnificent stained-glass windows awaits you in the abbey church.

Above: historic Chartres

Most of the old town is a protected site, and has been well restored. Chartres is also a lively agricultural centre and capital of the Beauce region. You can tour the city with a guide. Information, maps, books and brochures are available at the tourist office on Rue du Cloître Notre-Dame, beside the cathedral.

3. GIVERNY *(see pull-out map)*

This suggestion for a day trip takes you into Normandy, just a short distance northwest of Paris. Add adventure to your trip by setting out on a bicycle; SNCF French Railways offer rentals right at the station.

It's a little more difficult to reach **Giverny** than the previous destinations, but it is well worth the effort nonetheless. Take a train from the Gare St Lazare to Vernon, with a journey time of about an hour. Note that trains are quite infrequent, so ensure you check times in advance (for SNCF central reservations and information tel: 08 36 35 35 35, open 7am–10pm daily or check www.sncf.fr). At Vernon station, you can take a taxi or hop on a bike for the trip to **Claude Monet's House and Garden** at Giverny (1 April to 31 October only 10am–6pm, closed Monday). The pink-and-green house is an explosion of colour. The dining room is bright yellow, and the walls are covered with priceless china. The kitchen is a soaring sky blue. The walls of the artists' rooms are hung with Japanese prints from his extensive collection.

The gardens are Monet's paintings come to life. Here are the subjects of so many of his Impressionist works: the waterlilies, the Japanese bridge, the willow and pond. Not far away is the **Musée Américain** (1 April to 31 October only 10am–6pm, closed Monday), which charts the impact that Monet and the other Impressionists made on American art.

Giverny is very popular on summer afternoons, so start out early on a weekday to get the most pleasure from your visit. The Seine meets the river Epte here, and there are pretty spots for picnics. If you have a car, continue northwest to **Lyons la Forêt**, a village set in a beech forest. Potted geraniums decorate the windows of typical Normandy half-timbered facades. Otherwise, there are a couple of decent restaurants in Vernon.

4. DISNEYLAND PARIS *(see pull-out map)*

Disneyland Paris (open year round; hours are seasonal but generally 10am–6pm, Monday to Friday; 9am–8am Saturday and Sunday) is one of two overseas location for Disney outside the US – the other is in Tokyo, Japan. It is situated at Marne la Vallée 32km (20 miles) east of Paris and can be reached by either car or RER line A from central Paris at Auber, Châtelet or Étoile. Marne-la-Vallée is also linked up to the high-

speed TGV and there is a Eurostar train direct from London's Waterloo station.

Disneyland Paris was located on this site because of its centrality within Europe: potential venues in the UK and Spain were discounted because of more difficult access. French reaction to the arrival of Disney was mixed – even though Disney researchers had identified Walt himself as originating from the town of Isigny (D'Isigny = Disney).

Huge though the park is, it is still being developed, and in its final form it will cover an area one-fifth the size of Paris. In 1992. the first year of operation, twice as many people visited Disneyland Paris as climbed the Eiffel Tower or visited the Louvre. Even so, these numbers were lower than Disney had hoped, and some plans were rescheduled. Now, however, the park has been deemed a success by all. The park's official language is English, but French is widely spoken.

Entrance fees vary according to the season, and families with children should consider spreading their visit over two days. Disneyland Paris *passeports* are available in Paris at FNAC stores, the tourist office, the Disney store and Virgin Megastore on the Champs Elysées. To make reservations in one of Disneyland Paris's six hotels, telephone Paris 01 60 30 60 53 or 0990 030303 in the UK. The website address is disneylandparis.com. The on-site hotels can be expensive, but guests get early access to the attractions.

World of Magic

Disneyland Paris is similar to its US sisters. Disney's 'imagineers' have created five worlds: Fantasyland, the most popular land for younger children; Main Street USA, representing the early 1900s with ragtime and Dixieland bands; Frontierland, evoking dreams of the Wild West; Adventureland, with characters like Captain Hook; and futuristic Discoveryland, which has Space Mountain and several attractions with a French theme, such as Les Mystères de Nautilus, an underwater trip that pays homage to French sci-fi writer Jules Verne's *20,000 Leagues Under the Sea*. The rides and re-creations are very exciting – even queuing here can be great entertainment.

Left: Monet's house at Giverny
Above: Mickey Mouse and gang at Disneyland Paris

Leisure Activities

SHOPPING

Duty Free Regulations

US residents may take back $400 worth of merchandise per traveller for personal use or as gifts, before paying a flat 10 percent tax on additional value up to $1,000. Included in this allowance is 1 litre of alcohol per traveller over the age of 21 and one bottle of US-trademarked perfume. There is no tax on art or antiques more than 100 years old. Families may pool their declarations, provided that no similar ones have been made in the preceding 30-day period. Canadian residents have a $300 yearly limit, in addition to the 50 cigars, 200 cigarettes, 2lb of tobacco and 40fl oz of alcohol they may bring in tax free.

Duty-free was was abolished in 1999 for travel between European Union countries, and this open-door policy will eventually be accompanied by the standardisation of VAT. Meanwhile, prices (particularly for things like alcohol and cigarettes) are remarkably different in neighbouring countries. This has resulted in a fair amount of informal import and export, and has also encouraged the black-market sale of goods, particularly alcohol, in the UK.

Technically, there is no limit to the amount of goods you can bring into the UK from France providing tax has already been paid on them, but they must be for personal consumption. The term 'for personal use' is interpreted as being a maximum of 800 cigarettes, 400 cigarillos, 200 cigars, 1kg of smoking tobacco, 10 litres of spirits, 20 litres of fortified wines, 90 litres of wine, and 110 litres of beer. If you want to go over this limit to buy wine, say, for a wedding, it is advisable to take documentation to back up your story.

For non EU travellers entitled to buy duty-free, the tax-free outlets at the points of departure – for instance, those at the Eurostar terminal, in airports and on planes and boats – are not always the cheapest places to shop.

The mark-up, which can be as much as 100–200 percent, can sometimes overwhelm the tax savings, and you may find you would have been better off getting your duty-free goods from a regular shop in town. At this point you will have to decide whether it is worth reclaiming the duty that will be included in the price.

Only certain shops offer an instant refund on tax. In addition to Galeries Lafayette and Printemps department stores, **Raoul & Curly** at 47 Avenue de l'Opéra offers this service. To receive the refund you will need to take your plane ticket and passport to the shop to prove you will be taking the goods out of the country.

The other alternative is to get the VAT (TVA in France) refunded at the airport. To qualify for this procedure, your purchases in a single store must amount to 1,200 francs for non-EU residents. The store must fill out a special form (make sure it corresponds to your place of residence). You must include

Left: Parisian elegance in the Galerie Colbert
Right: Parisian dolls waiting for a home

and a satisfactory selection of alcoholic drinks; luxury shops on the Place de la Madeleine offer high-quality items in gift packages. **Perfumes** are another favourite purchase, but the prices are only interesting if you can buy them tax-free.

Beauty and Fashion

Fashion is synonymous with Paris, and just looking at Parisians makes you want to dress up. The venerable couture houses are on Avenue Montaigne and Faubourg St Honoré. Ironically, the capital of *haute couture* is increasingly dominated by foreign designers; the Japanese have injected a note of originality with such names as Kenzo and Issey Miyake (3 Place des Vosges), while German Karl Lagerfield has long masterminded design at Chanel.

For more affordable, ready-to-wear designer fashion, as well as accessories and cosmetics, head for **Le Bon Marché Rive Gauche** department store on Rue de Sèvres (Metro: Sèvres-Babylone), where you'll find the best representation of French taste, the epitome of French *art de vivre*. More affordable clothes can be found around St Germain and the streets around St Sulpice where, alongside the prêt-à-porter boutiques of up-and-coming designers, are international chains such as Gap and shops selling fashionable items for the home.

Les Halles has a wide selection of shops, including a good selection of teenage fashion.

banking information on the form, because refunds are only paid directly into accounts. Customs officials will ask for the forms when you leave France, and they will look at the goods, so be sure to allow plenty of time. In general, it is not worth the hassle to seek a refund this way, unless you've got an expensive item to declare.

Alcohol and Perfumes

If you want to buy **alcohol**, I suggest you stick with liqueurs, apéritifs or champagnes. Good wine may suffer on the journey and end up disappointing you. Also, French wine is so competitively priced around the world, you'd do better to buy back home. Major supermarkets in Paris have the best prices

shopping

Nearby Rue du Jour has dozens of shops selling new and used clothing for men and women.

Look for *Soldes*, seasonal sales often held in December and June. *Liquidation* means 'everything must go'. Women's and men's clothes are sized from 36 (small) to 48 (extra large). Shoes start at 36 (UK size 3) through 46 (UK size 12). Children's clothes are marked by age, but sizes tend to be less generous than in the UK; baby shoes start at 19. My advice is to try items on.

To find everyday things that you need while travelling, whether shampoo, a warm sweater, an insole for your shoe or a sketch pad for your drawings, try one of the many branches of the less expensive department store **Monoprix**. These stores are located all over town and smaller and less crowded than the major department stores. Most also offer shoe and clothing repair services and have one floor of grocery items. Clean, inexpensive and well organised, they offer good-quality merchandise and are pleasant to shop in. The large branch of the perfume chain **Séphora** on the Champs Elysées sells an amazing array of perfumes, make-up products and other toiletries. Smaller specialised boutiques also offer sophisticated products and perfumes as well as services such as manicure, hair removal and facial massage in their **Salons de Beauté**.

Hair Salons

Hairdressers are easy enough to locate, but always busy. One of the most popular salons is **Jacques Dessange**, with several locations across the city. Call the Franklin Roosevelt salon, tel: 01 43 59 31 31, for information and an appointment. Another favourite chain is **Jean Louis David** (tel: 01 42 97 50 08), with 14 salons and a beauty school offering discount prices on modern styles.

The more exclusive **Maniatis** has three salons: 18 Rue Marbeuf (tel: 01 47 23 30 14) near the Champs Elysées, and 35 Rue de Sèvres (tel: 01 45 44 16 39) and 12 Rue du Four (tel: 01 46 34 79 83), both near St Germain des Prés.

Souvenirs

The boutique **Chic et Choc** in Les Halles Metro station is worth a look. They have all sorts of items with the Paris Metro logo. Another special spot is the **Réunion des Musées Nationaux**, 10 Rue de l'Abbaye, near St Germain-des-Prés. They offer posters and catalogues from Paris museums, dating back to 1966. On a higher price scale, try the **Louvre des Antiquaires**, 2 Place du Palais Royal, for antique furnishings, prints and paintings. Some of the dealers here have less expensive shops elsewhere, so ask for a card.

Markets

Adventurous visitors and determined bargain hunters may choose to head for **flea markets** to dig out something unique. The most well known of these markets is the Puces de Saint-Ouen at **Porte de Clignan-**

court (Saturday to Monday 7am–7.30pm; Metro: Porte de Clignancourt).

In the city, try the **Marché d'Aligre**, a food and flower market, which also has a section of old books, clothes, glassware, lace and jewellery (Place d'Aligre, near Bastille, Metro: Ledru-Rollin; closed Monday).

Of the markets held outside the city, the best for bargains is the **Marché de Montreuil** to the east (Metro: Porte de Montreuil). Old clothes, junk and genuine finds all day Saturday, Sunday and Monday.

A few other suggestions for gifts or treats that are easy to pack and take home include: perfumed soaps in decorative boxes (available from pharmacies); chocolates in pretty packets, sold in bakeries and *confiseries*, Dijon mustard and various types of French vinegar packaged in attractive jars and bottles; 'Perfumes of Paris' collections with sample sizes, on sale in many of the smaller beauty product boutiques.

Above left: window-shopping in the Rue de Rivoli
Left: Parisian refinement on display. **Above:** for designer labels

EATING OUT

It would take years to sample all the restaurants in Paris, and a staff to keep up with changes and openings. Parisians enjoy eating at their favourite *bistro* as much as discovering a new restaurant or having a night out in a really fine establishment. Take the suggestions given in each itinerary in this book, or walk into a place that looks (and smells) great, or just try the restaurants listed below. Addresses include the *code postal*, of which the last two numbers indicate the district (*arrondissement*). Prices are based on the set price menu, if there is one, or a three-course *à la carte* meal for one person, with a moderately priced wine.

Many restaurants close on Sunday. Reservations are required in expensive restaurants, and are highly recommended on Friday and Saturday nights for moderate restaurants.

The price of dinner may vary, especially if you order a special bottle of wine or champagne. Lunch is served from noon until about 2pm. Dinner service starts around 8pm. Brasseries serve a limited menu (eggs, hot ham sandwiches, sausages) all day; cafés generally have cold sandwiches on crusty baguettes of bread at any hour. If you want a super gourmet experience, try lunchtime rather than dinner, when many expensive places have set menus that can offer real savings over *à la carte*.

Expensive Restaurants

Dinner with a moderately priced wine cost at least 700 francs per person. Lunch tend to be much cheaper, especially for set menus

Arpège
84 Rue de Varenne (75007)
Tel: 01 45 51 47 33
Closed Sat, Sun lunch, and middle two week of August; credit cards: American Express Diners Club, Mastercard and Visa
This superb restaurant is among the top 1 in Paris. The wine-cellar is particularly good and not expensive. Expect to pay between 700 and 1,000 francs, excluding wine.

Hôtel Costes
239 Rue St-Honoré (75001)
Tel: 01 42 44 50 25
Open daily till 1am; all credit cards
The chic and trendy restaurant of Hôtel Costes is the place to see and be seen. Stars models and other VIPs seem to play their own part in this incredible kitsch setting. The cooking, however, is classical, and you'll pay around 500 francs per person. Advanced booking is essential.

Lasserre
17 Av Franklin Roosevelt (75008)
Tel: 01 43 59 53 43
Closed on Sunday, Monday lunch and in August; no credit cards
In the summer, you dine under the stars when they roll back the roof upstairs. There is an incredible wine list, and the dishes are rather on the delicate side. Just using the cutlery is half the pleasure of dining here. You'll pay around 900 francs per person.

Maison Blanche
15, Av Montaigne (75008)
Tel: 01 47 23 55 99
Fax: 01 47 20 09 56
Closed on Saturday and Monday for lunch and on Sunday; credit cards: American Express, Mastercard and Visa
Dining on the rooftop of the Champs-Elysées

Left: a ring-side seat

Theatre, you have a breathtaking view over the Seine and the rest of Paris, along with the finest French cooking, which is classical, refined and very light. Ask for a table by the picture window or on the terrace in summer, and expect to pay a minimum of 750 francs per person.

Taillevent
15 Rue Lamennais (75008)
Tel: 01 44 95 15 01
Credit cards: American Express, Diners Club, Mastercard, Visa
Fine French cuisine in wood-panelled surroundings. This is one of the best restaurants in Paris. Exceptional wine list. Around 900 francs per person.

La Tour d'Argent
15 Quai de la Tournelle (75005)
Tel: 01 43 54 23 31
Closed on Monday; credit cards: American Express, Diners Club, Mastercard and Visa
Famous for the view of Notre Dame as well as its recipes based on duck. The service is impeccable, the décor divine. Expect to pay at least 900 francs per person for dinner.

Moderate Restaurants

There is an abundance of restaurants in this category, where a meal for one with wine costs between 230 and 350 francs. The following are a few favourites:

Auberge de Jarente
7 Rue de Jarente (75004)
Tel: 01 42 77 49 35
Closed Sunday, Monday and for the whole of August; credit cards: American Express, Diners Club and Visa
A small but welcoming restaurant specialising in the kind of uncomplicated cuisine that makes a welcome change from some French establishments. Both the *pipérade de St Jean* and the *gâteau Basque* can be recommended.

Le Bar des Théâtres
6 Av Montaigne (75008)
Tel: 01 47 23 34 63
Open daily; credit card: Visa
This busy, noisy place has been around for more than 40 years, serving tasty and traditional French food in a friendly atmosphere. It has its drawbacks: don't mind the napkins, and keep away if you hate cigarette smoke while you're eating. However, on the positive side, this place typifies the kind of restaurant that used to make people say it was impossible to get a bad meal in France.

Le Basilic
2 Rue Casimir-Périer (75007)
Tel: 01 44 18 94 64
Open daily except Christmas week; credit cards: Visa, Mastercard, American Express
On a quiet square of the 7th district overlooking St-Clotilde Church, a classical, comfortable *brasserie* in which to rest after visiting the Invalides and the Rodin Museum.

Le Café Marly
Palais du Louvre
93 Rue de Rivoli (75001)
Tel: 01 49 26 06 60
Open daily, 8am–2am; all credit cards
Located in the former Ministry of Finance apartments in the Palais du Louvre, these Napoleon III staterooms, with black and golden ceilings, now house a very fashionable restaurant. For a break during – or after – a visit to the museum, try this simple, up-to-date cooking.

Le Domarais
53 bis, Rue des Francs-Bourgeois (75004)
Tel: 01 42 74 54 17
Closed on Sunday and at the end of August;

Above: La Tour d'Argent

credit cards: American Express and Visa
The Marais' dome, as referred to in the name, comprises an astonishing round hall with high vaulted ceiling, a former chapel, and what was, two centuries ago, the main hall of the Mont-de-Piété (Paris credit institution). Its white, golden and dark red décor makes it a beautiful environment for the fresh inventive cooking.

Chez Ma Cousine
12 Rue Norvins (75018)
Tel: 01 46 06 49 35
Open daily; credit cards: American Express, Diners Club, Mastercard and Visa
Located in Montmartre, right on the Place du Tertre, this small and friendly restaurant also offers a cabaret in the evening. If you want faster food, it has a *crêpe* stand on the street that serves the passing traffic.

Chez Paul
15 Place Dauphine (75001)
Tel: 01 43 54 21 48
Closed on Monday; credit cards: all except Diners Club
Have you ever dreamed of being in Paris in a quintessential Gallic restaurant with red-and-white chequered tablecloths, overlooking one of the city's nicest squares? Well, *Chez Paul*, located on the old royal Place Dauphine just behind the Pont Neuf, fits the bill. You'll eat the same French dishes as those cooked for actors Yves Montand and Simone Signoret.

China Club
50 Rue de Charenton (75012)
Tel: 01 43 43 82 02
Open daily; credit cards: American Express and Visa
Just behind the Opéra Bastille, China Club has a wonderful ambience in the restaurant and a bar open until the early hours (2am in the week, 3.30am on Saturday and Sunday). You'll feel like you're in the exotic atmosphere of 1930s Shanghai as you enjoy Chinese food to the accompaniment of classical music. Sophisticated and serene.

La Citrouille
10 Rue Grégoire de Tours (75006)
Tel: 01 43 29 90 41
Open daily
Located in the heart of the Latin Quarter on the famous Left Bank near Odéon, this restaurant serves excellent fresh salads and simple but well-prepared dishes at very reasonable prices. Come here for a pleasant escape from steak and French fries.

Da Graziano
83 Rue Lepic (75018)
Tel: 01 46 06 84 77
Open daily; credit cards: Eurocard, Mastercard and Visa
Unbelievable setting that is both kitsch and charming, just below the old Moulin de la Galette. The Italian food is delicious, the service attentive and professional, and the proprietor is the brother of singer Dalida.

La Méditerranée
2 Place de l'Odéon (75006)
Tel: 01 43 26 02 30
Open daily; credit cards: American Express, Mastercard and Visa
A fish restaurant whose frescoes were painted in the 1940s and 1950s by decorator Christian Bérard and whose logo was designed by Jean Cocteau. Artists, writers, comedians of the Odéon Theatre and neighbouring senators are familiar with this landmark of French Mediterranean cooking. Seafood, bouillabaisse or bass carpaccio? – a gourmet's dilemma.

Natacha
17 bis, Rue Campagne-Première (75014)
Tel: 01 43 20 79 27
Closed on Sunday and in August; credit cards: American Express and Visa
Smart, selective, classical and open only in the evening. This is the place to see actors and movie stars, and dine at midnight behind the red curtains.

Above: you can find excellent seafood in Paris

Le Petit Robert

10 Rue Cauchois (75018)
Tel: 01 46 06 04 46
Closed on Sunday, Monday and in August;
credit cards: all except American Express
Located in the real Montmartre, a quiet and
refined location to sample and appreciate
the ever-traditional cuisine of southwestern
France.

Pierrot

18 Rue Etienne Marcel (75002)
Tel: 01 45 08 00 10
Located near Les Halles, Pierrot is known
for its pâtés and wines, excellent French
cooking and friendly service.

La Régalade

49 Av Jean Moulin (75014)
Tel: 01 45 45 68 58
Closed on Saturday for lunch, Sunday, Mon-
day, from mid-July to mid-August, and
Christmas week; credit cards: Mastercard
and Visa
This is one of the best places to eat in the
whole of Paris, discreet and delicious, and
situated not far from Metro Alesia. The chef
is Basque, as is his cooking, which is simple but outstanding. Booking is highly recommended.

Square Trousseau

1 Rue Antoine-Vollon (75012)
Tel: 01 43 43 06 00
Closed for Christmas and New Year's Day;
credit cards: American Express and Visa
Overlooking the exquisite Square Trousseau,
behind the Bastille, this restaurant has a sophisticated Parisian atmosphere, and French
cooking with fresh seasonal food.

Terminus Nord

23 Rue de Dunkerque (75010)
Tel: 01 42 85 05 15
Open daily, 11am–12.30am; credit cards:
American Express, Diners Club, Mastercard
and Visa
Just across from the Gare du Nord station,
this big, busy brasserie has a 1925 décor and
a staff of very professional waiters. It specialises in traditional French food and hearty
portions, with first-rate seafood, and excellent beef and lamb dishes.

Right: enjoying a beer, Paris-style

Le Train Bleu

Gare de Lyon
20 Blvd Diderot (75012)
Tel: 01 43 43 09 06
Fax: 01 43 43 97 96
Open daily; all credit cards
Inside the Gare de Lyon, this Belle Epoque
restaurant is as beautiful as it is original. The
paintings on the walls depict all the towns the
trains travel through, creating a wonderful atmosphere in which to enjoy the traditional
French cooking.

Inexpensive Restaurants

For less than 200 francs per person, you can
have the pleasure of a good French meal with
wine at the following establishments:

Café Charbon

109 Rue Oberkampf (75011)
Tel: 01 43 57 55 13
Open daily, 9am–2am; credit cards: all ex-
cept American Express
A stone's throw from Place de la République,
this is a trendy Parisian *bistrot* serving such
classic dishes as *côte de bœuf*. Very tasty.

Café de la Mairie

8 Place St Sulpice (75006)
No credit cards
Left Bank eatery undiscovered by most
tourists. A genuine piece of France.

Chartier

7 Rue du Faubourg Montmartre (75009)
Tel: 01 47 70 86 29
Closed Sunday
Located near the Opéra, this is the best-known
low-price restaurant in town. The ambience

dishes as *gratin dauphinoise* or *andouillettes*. Specialises in Lyonnais cuisine.

La Palette
43 Rue de Seine (75006)
Tel: 01 43 26 68 15
Open daily 8am–2pm, closed on Sunday, holy days and in August; all credit cards
This is an authentic Parisian bistro which manages to retain an indefinable charm. Relaxed and comfortable.

Au Pain Quotidien
18 Place du Marché St-Honoré (75001)
3 Rue Bachaumont (75002)
18 Rue des Archives (75004)
Open daily, 7am–7pm; credit cards: American Express, Mastercard and Visa
You can have breakfast, salads, invigorating *tartines* as well as tea and supper served round the clock at this friendly *table d'hôte*. A very good idea, especially when you're a tourist and need to get your strength back after some serious sightseeing. Low prices.

Le Parc aux Cerfs
50 Rue Vavin (75006)
Tel: 01 43 54 87 83
Open daily, closed in August; credit cards: Visa and Eurocard
A refined bistro with retro lamplights, next door to Montparnasse. Very good value: first-rate service and a modern, light style of French cooking.

Pastavino
59 Rue Dauphine (75006)
and 30 Rue Passy (75016)
For a change from French food, this Italian restaurant and take-away serves salads, pasta dishes and tasty desserts at unbeatable prices. More branches will be opening.

Polidor
41 Rue Monsieur-le-Prince (75006)
Tel: 01 43 26 95 34
No credit cards
Favoured by students and professors, this Latin Quarter hangout offers home-style cooking and Art Deco design. Everything is very relaxed, including the service, and no gastronomic miracles are in order, but Hemingway ate here, and so can you.

is an experience in itself: there is 1890s décor; the waiters are snappy and the tables are shared; there is plenty of bonhomie. Arrive before 2pm, or 9.30pm for dinner, or you probably won't get a seat.

Le Comptoir du Relais
5 Carrefour de l'Odéon (75006)
Tel: 01 43 29 12 05
Open daily; no credit cards
The *bistrot* of Hôtel Relais Saint-Germain at Carrefour de l'Odéon is open until midnight during the week, and until 2am on Friday and Saturday night. Go whenever you feel hungry for a piece of pie, a glass of good wine and a great atmosphere.

Les Fous de l'Ile
33 Rue des Deux-Ponts (75004)
Tel: 01 43 25 76 67
Closed on Monday, Sunday evening; credit cards: Mastercard and Visa
Friendly, simple and warm. A fine ambience and unpretentious cooking in the heart of the Ile St-Louis. On Tuesday evening there is a concert after dinner, and Sunday is the day for brunch. The restaurant functions as a tearoom in the afternoon.

Le Mâchon d'Henri
8 Rue Guisarde (75006)
Tel: 01 43 29 08 70
Open daily; no credit cards accepted
Beams and stone, and a warm authentic setting are the order of the day for this excellent bistro serving such classic French

Above: Paris by night

Le Temps des Cerises
131 Rue de la Cerisaie (75004)
Tel: 01 42 72 08 63
Closed Saturday, Sunday and in August
Lunch only
A modest family-run restaurant in the Marais, by the Bastille. Simple working-men's food. Excellent value.

In addition, remember that all the **Flo Prestige** brasseries (**Le Balzar, Bofinger, La Coupole, Terminus Nord**, etc) offer a special 'Night Hunger' menu from 10.30pm, for 138 francs (wine included).

Bars and Wine Bars

Brasserie de l'Ile St Louis
55 Quai de Bourbon (75004)
Tel: 01 43 54 02 59
Closed during August
Lively Alsatian brasserie.

L'Ecluse
15 Quai des Grands-Augustins (75006)
Rue Mondétour (75001)
Rue du Pont Lodi (75006)
Place de la Madeleine (75008)
Rue François 1er (75008)
All branches closed Sunday
L'Ecluse is the granddaddy of all Parisian wine bars, and its popularity shows no signs of diminishing. Although it is fairly expensive, it offers a truly outstanding selection of Bordeaux wines, plus a range of appetising snacks to accompany them.

Harry's New York Bar
5 Rue Daunou (75002)
Tel: 01 42 61 71 14
I couldn't leave this one out. Harry's opened in 1911, was virtually a second home to Hemingway, and the Bloody Mary was created here. Still popular today, it attracts plenty of interesting characters. Open until late.

Juvéniles
47 Rue de Richelieu (75001)
Tel: 01 42 97 46 49
Closed on Sunday and holy days; credit cards: all except American Express
A Scot owns this friendly wine bar; tapas and curries are served with a wide selection of wine, sherry and – of course – Scottish malt.

Le Passage
18 Passage de la Bonne-Graine (75011)
Tel: 01 47 00 73 30
Closed Saturday lunch and Sunday; credit cards: American Express and Visa
Behind the Bastille, next door to the Rue du Faubourg Saint-Antoine, a charming French wine restaurant. Their wine bar, **Le Café du Passage** (12, Rue de Charonne), is open daily from 6pm to 2am.

Le Rubis
10 Rue du Marché St Honoré (75001)
Tel: 01 42 61 03 14
Closed weekends and during August; no credit cards
This is the place to be when the Beaujolais Nouveau comes out in October and the party that assembles fills up the whole street. At other times of the year, it is a pleasant place for lunch with a glass of something divine. Popular *plats du jour* include *bœuf bourguignon* and lentils with salt pork (*petit salé aux lentilles*).

Le Vin des Rues
21 Rue Boulard (75014)
Tel: 01 43 22 19 78
Open from Tuesday to Saturday for lunch, dinner on Wednesday and Friday, closed on Sunday, Monday and in August; credit cards: American Express and Visa
Delicious and genuine wine restaurant. The setting has remained the same for years, the traditional cooking is from Lyon and the wine list is written down on the blackboard. English may not be spoken but you'll really feel at home here.

Willi's Wine Bar
13 Rue des Petits-Champs (75001)
Tel: 01 42 61 05 09
Closed on Sunday;
credit cards: Mastercard and Visa
Chic and warm, attracting a mixture of businessmen and people from the world of fashion. There's an English bar with a great selection of French wines, mainly from the Rhône Valley, as well as good hearty dishes and a magnificent cheeseboard.

Right: at your service

NIGHTLIFE

There's plenty to do in Paris after the street-lights come on. Expect a late start in summer.

River Trips

The **Vedettes du Pont Neuf** (entrance under the Pont Neuf off Place Dauphine) leave roughly every 30 minutes until 5pm Monday to Thursday, and until 10pm during the rest of the week. The trip takes about an hour and powerful spotlights illuminate the bridges and buildings as you go. The same tours are run by **Bateaux Mouches** at Pont de l'Alma, although not quite as frequently. Across from the Eiffel Tower at the Pont d'Iéna are **Les Bateaux Parisiens**, which also offer gastronomic cruises.

Nocturnal Bus Tours

These pass the spendidly illuminated monuments of the city. Some end at the Moulin Rouge for French can-can and champagne, or the Lido on the Champs-Elysées. Two well-known tours in town are **Paris Vision** (214 Rue de Rivoli 75001) and **Cityrama** (149 Rue St Honoré 75001); their packages are also sold in many agencies, and most hotels carry their leaflets. Both companies also organise day trips to popular sites such as Versailles, Giverny, Disneyland Paris and Chartres.

Music and Theatre

Tickets to the ballet, opera, concerts, or theatre productions can be bought at an agency or at the theatre itself. The FNAC stores (music and books) around town (there's a main branch in the Forum des Halles shopping centre) sell tickets to most concerts. For theatrical productions, go to the Kiosque de la Madeleine, a big ticket booth in the middle of Place de la Madeleine, or to the Kiosque Montparnasse, in front of the station. You can buy half-price tickets on the day. For the **Opéra de Paris**, call their booking office (tel: 08 36 69 78 98). Booking is also possible on the web: www.opera-de-paris.fr.

Complete weekly listings are in *L'Officiel des Spectacles*, *Pariscope* and other magazines. Also look out for Paris's distinctive green 'Morris columns' on street corners, which are usually splashed with posters.

Jazz Clubs

Paris loves jazz, and the clubs seem to have undergone a renaissance recently. Check the listings in the magazine *L'Officiel des Spectacles* to see what's on in the following clubs.

Jazz Club Lionel Hampton
Hotel Meridien
81 Blvd Gouvion-St Cyr (75017)
A favourite with performers and fans. Seats several hundred. Run by a local jazz hero known simply as Moustache, the club has hosted some of the world's finest jazz musicians, such as Harry Edison, Oscar Peterson, Memphis Slim and Benny Carter. If you're not a night owl, you can enjoy jazz here on Sunday, over brunch.

New Morning
7–9 Rue des Petits Ecuries (75010)
Tel: 01 45 23 51 41
Big with scant décor. Some of the greats, including Richie Havens, Taj Mahal, Wayne Shorter, Stan Getz and Prince have returned a number of times. Informal and hip.

Le Petit Journal
71 Blvd St Michel (75005) and
Le Petit Journal Montparnasse
13 Rue du Commandant-Mouchotte (75014)
Same owners, but different styles. The St

Michel version offers Dixieland and swing; the Montparnasse club has featured more modern legends such as Herbie Hancock and Stéphane Grappelli. Good food and vibes.

Nightclubs

Clubs in Paris tend to be very 'clubby' and they subject would-be partiers to heavy scrutiny at the door. Dress fashionably, bring plenty of money, and don't forget to smile.

Les Bains
7 Rue du Bourg-l'Abbé (75003)
Tel: 01 48 87 01 80
This old public bathhouse is the gathering place of fashion victims and the young and trendy. To be sure of getting in, make a reservation at the restaurant first.

Le Balajo
9 Rue de Lappe (75011)
Tel: 01 47 00 07 87
A popular venue attracting a chic crowd with its Latin music. Open Thursday and Sunday afternoon, Thursday to Sunday evening.

La Locomotive
90 Boulevard de Clichy (75018)
Tel: 08 36 69 69 28
Rough, ready, mainstream, enormous.

Au Neo
21 Rue Montorgeuil (75001)
A cellar club that attracts a mix of customers on its varied evenings.

Above: welcome to the club
Right: blowing up a storm

Le Queen
102 Av des Champs-Elysées (75008)
Tel: 01 53 89 08 90
Website: www.queen.fr
The biggest trendy club in Paris is actually a gay club but it opens its doors to anyone in a festive mood who looks the part. Monday is a 'disco inferno' evening, Wednesday is a 'French touch' straight evening, Thursday is openly gay, Friday and Saturday are dedicated to international house music, and Sunday is a kitsch evening devoted to the sounds of the 1980s.

Le Tango
11 Rue au Maire (75003)
Meeting place for African *sapeurs*: guys who spend fantastic sums of money on incredible clothes. You have a wild time in store, if you're dressed right.

CALENDAR OF EVENTS

The main tourist season in Paris is from June until September, and Easter is also a very busy period. July and August are big holiday months for the French, so a number of shops, restaurants and theatres are closed. However, there is still plenty for visitors to see, including summer festivals, sound-and-light shows, and extravagant fireworks displays, and there is a happy and relaxed atmosphere in the city streets, which are less crowded than at other times of the year.

National holidays (*jours fériés*) mean closed banks and heavy traffic, so plan around the following:

1 January *Jour de l'An*
Easter Monday *Lundi de Pâques*
1 May *Fête du Travail*
8 May *Victoire 1945*
Ascension Day *L'Ascension*
Whit Monday *Pentecôte*
14 July *Fête Nationale* (**Bastille Day**)
15 August *L'Assomption*
1 November *La Toussaint*
11 November *L'Armistice 1918*
25 December *Noël*

When packing seasonable clothes for your holiday, bear in mind that the French, and especially Parisians, like to dress up to go to work, out to dinner, or to the theatre. It's fine to wear jeans when visiting museums, but they are frowned upon in many restaurants and expensive shops.

January–March

The weather is cold and damp, and the only advantages of this period are lower fares and hotel rates, and thinner crowds at the museums. The 'Printemps des Musées', a cultural campaign running through March, will enable you to discover museum collections usually kept in the reserves; you may be shown around by the curator himself.

April–May

Springtime in Paris is a legend, of course, and one the city usually lives up to, if only for a fleeting moment. Temperatures lie in the 16–22°C (60–72°F) range. The days lengthen deliciously as heavy chestnut blooms appear against unfurling green foliage. If you are lucky with your timing, Paris in these months can be at its most enchanting.

The sporting highlights include the Paris Marathon in April and the French Open Tennis Championship at the end of May in the Roland-Garros stadium.

June–July

In the early part of the summer there are many celebrations. To begin with, the 'Fête de la Musique', on 21 June, is one big street party: everybody is out celebrating the first day of summer while music plays all over the city;

a carnival atmosphere prevails. Other musical events at this time include the Montmartre Jazz Festival and a series of classical concerts at the Sorbonne.

Bastille Day, known in France as La Fête Nationale, is on 14 July. The party begins with a morning military parade down the Champs Elysées, continues with fireworks over the Eiffel Tower and dancing till dawn at the various Firemen's Balls. Be careful to watch out for the sizzling firecrackers!

The Tour de France bicycle race sprints to a finish on the Champs Elysées around the end of the fourth week of July.

August

Thousands of Parisians leave the city in August for their annual holidays, and the city slows down as a result. Visit the fair in the Tuileries Park and go on the big Ferris wheel for a thrilling view. Look out for the 'Paris Quartier d'Eté' programme: the city offers a multicultural outdoors festival – with dance, music and theatre – in wonderful settings and at very low cost.

September

This period is called *la rentrée* – the return. To celebrate the event, the 'Fêtes de la Seine' bring enchantment to the great river with breathtaking fireworks. On the second weekend of this month, the Palais de l'Elysée, the ministries and other monuments usually closed to the public open their doors for free during 'Les Journées du Patrimoine'. So do private gardens during the 'Fête des Jardins de Paris' at about the same time.

Also in September are: new fashions; a major art show, the Foire Internationale de l'Art Contemporain (FIAC); plus new productions from the worlds of theatre, music, dance and film in the Paris Autumn Festival, running through to December.

October–November

October and November are wine months, with the Montmartre harvest festival and the arrival of Beaujolais Nouveau (the first Thursday after 15 November). It is also time for the Prix de l'Arc de Triomphe; and the famous Paris–Deauville vintage car run.

You can shake hands with your favourite

French author and even have a book dedicated to you during the numerous meetings of 'Lire en Fête'.

Every other year, November is also the 'Mois de la Photo' (the Month of the Photograph); a thematic selection of works are presented by the artists who have gathered together material specifically for this event.

The International Dance Festival continues throughout November, while churches are resounding with the 'Festival d'Art Sacré' concerts, which play until Christmas.

December

Christmas shopping starts at the end of November, and the streets are magnificent. The city has a bustling, busy quality in the days preceding the end-of-the-year holiday. The speciality food shops look particularly enticing at this time of year, with hams and cheeses to tempt all but the most puritan. You can even see wild boar hanging from hooks outside butchers' shops.

Christmas is traditionally a family affair, but New Year's Eve is a big party occasion.

For further information, you should check out the website of the Paris Tourist Office: www-paris-touristoffice.com. When in Paris, watch the public digital signposts at every crossroads which read 'La Mairie de Paris vous informe...', or phone the information desk (tel: 01 42 76 47 47).

Left: the Tour de France finishes in Paris in July
Above: national colours on Bastille Day

Practical
Information

GETTING THERE

By Plane

You can arrive at one of two airports serving Paris. To the north, **Charles de Gaulle** (tel: 01 48 62 22 80), also referred to as 'Roissy', is the bigger and more modern of the two. From there, you can take the RER line B to the Gare du Nord (every 15 minutes) or the Air France bus to the Arc de Triomphe. The Roissybus runs roughly every 15 minutes, 6am–11pm, between the airport and the Place de l'Opéra, taking about 45 minutes. A taxi takes about 40–50 minutes to reach the centre, and costs about 250 francs. Add another 30 minutes for a rush-hour journey.

Orly is the other major Parisian airport (tel: 01 49 75 15 15), to the south of Paris, and it handles mostly domestic flights and charter flights. Air France buses travel between Orly and the Invalides Terminal. This is a convenient drop-off place, where you can board either the Metro or RER directly. The Air France buses then continue on to Gare Montparnasse.

A city bus (Orlybus) comes into the southern end of Paris at the Denfert-Rochereau Metro station every 15 minutes. A taxi takes 30–40 minutes (but much longer during rush hour), and costs about 25 euros (€).

By Train

Eurostar: since the opening of the Channel Tunnel in 1995, you can travel by rail between central London (Waterloo) and central Paris (Gare du Nord) in just three hours.

Various special tickets and cheap deals are offered on the Eurostar service: ask what is available when you make your booking. In theory, tickets can be booked up to 30 minutes before departure, but in practice the cheap tickets (especially at the weekend, even in the low season) get booked up early.

Check-in closes 20 minutes before the train leaves. For more information, contact Eurostar (tel: 0345 30 30 30).

Left: Art Nouveau Metro entrance
Right: confusing times, Gare St Lazare

TRAVEL ESSENTIALS

Visas

Travellers to France must have a valid passport. EU and American citizens do not need visas, but visitors from other countries should contact the nearest French consulate or a local tourist office.

Time

France is six hours ahead of US Eastern Standard time and one hour ahead of Greenwich Mean Time. The clocks move forward one hour at the end of March, and revert back one hour in October.

Electricity

Paris runs on 220 volts, 50 cycles. If you carry a travel iron or hair dryer, make sure you have an adaptor so that it will fit in the French socket. If you've forgotten to bring one along, you can buy one from an 'Electricité' or 'Quincaillerie' (hardware) shop.

MONEY MATTERS

Many banks in the city will change foreign cash or traveller's cheques, and there are no special differences in the rates. Banking

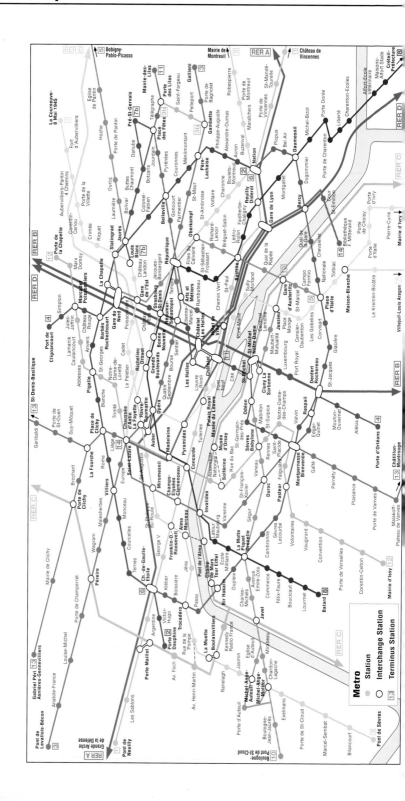

hours are 9am–5pm on weekdays. The exchange window at the Gare du Nord is open until midnight on weekdays, and other station banks are open until 8pm.

Cashpoint machines at the Opéra (the BNP Bank) and at No 66 on the Champs Elysées (BRED) will convert foreign bills into francs. The easiest way to draw cash is to use your credit or cashpoint/ATM card in the ATMs outside most banks. Avoid changing money at hotels, where exchange rates may be poor.

Hotline numbers for lost cards are as follows: American Express (tel: 01 47 77 72 00); Diners Club (tel: 01 49 06 17 50); Carte Bleu/Visa (tel: 08 36 69 08 80); Mastercard (tel: 08 00 90 13 87).

The basic unit of money is the euro (€), introduced as the official French currency in January 1999 and in everyday use from January 2002. The euro replaces the previous currency, the French franc (FF).

Tipping

Tipping is common in a number of places. In hotels, restaurants and cafés there is always a service charge, but people usually leave the small change from the bill in the saucer. Prices listed *prix nets* or *service compris* mean service is included. If the price says *service en sus* or *service non compris*, an extra 12–15 percent will be added to the total. A tip of around €1 is usually given to: room service waiters (except breakfast), ushers, washroom and cloakroom attendants. Taxi drivers and hairdressers expect about 15 percent.

GETTING AROUND

Paris has 20 *arrondissements* (districts) spiralling out from the Louvre. The last two numbers of the postal code (750XX) are the *arrondissement* number.

Driving

Driving in Paris is, generally speaking, a nightmare, typified by traffic jams, insults flying and a lack of parking spaces. Better to rely on the excellent public transport network. Or use your feet. If you insist on driving, remember to stay on the right-hand side of the road, to fasten seat belts in both the front and back of your vehicle, and to keep your

speed down to a maximum of 50km per hour (30mph) in town.

Metro, Buses and Trains

In the Metro, ask for a free map (*un plan du Métro*) and the guide *Paris Patchwork*.

You can travel on bus and Metro with tickets purchased at the ticket booth in any Metro station. These are much cheaper when you buy 10 at once (*un carnet*).

There is also a tourist card called *Paris Visite*, available for foreign visitors and valid for one to five days of unlimited travel on the Metro, bus (including to and from the airports), RER and suburban SNCF lines and Montmartre funicular. There are three types of *Paris Visite* available: for zones 1–3, zones 1–5 and zones 1–8, stretching as far as Versailles, Disneyland Paris or Fontainebleau. The ticket also gives discount admission to many tourist sites.

It is simple to use the Metro system, which is the densest in the world, with stops, on average, every 550m (180ft) or so. The lines are named after their terminal points, for example Château de Vincennes-Pont de Neuilly crosses the city from north to south, ending at those two stops. You can transfer between lines as many times as you need to on the same ticket, by following the orange signs marked *Correspondances* in the tunnels.

In general, the Metro has a reputation for being quite safe, although you should guard your wallet or purse carefully, especially when surrounded by big crowds and when travelling late at night.

Above: you're never far from a station

Trains run from 5.30am–12.30am. Follow the sign *Accès aux Quais* to reach the tracks, and *Sortie* to the street. Keep hold of your ticket until you exit the system: an inspector may want to check it.

Buses run on different schedules, but usually start around 6.30am and stop around 8.30pm. Only certain buses run on Sunday or late at night. Bus shelters all have maps and route information. When you board a bus, you must show your pass or punch a ticket in the machine by the driver.

If you can decipher public transport systems, the city buses are a great way to get around. The Balabus is particularly good for sightseeing, with 10 stops (marked *Bb*) between Gare du Lyon and La Grande Arche de La Défense.

The RER rail lines go out to the suburbs. They can be useful for crossing town quickly, and you can use a Metro ticket on the RER within the city. If travelling further out of the city, make sure your pass covers the area; if not, you must buy a more expensive ticket.

Taxis

Taxis are best found at taxi stands, clearly marked by large signs. You can also call a taxi company: Alpha Taxi (tel: 01 45 85 85 85); Taxis Bleus: (tel: 01 49 36 10 10); G7 Taxis (tel: 01 47 39 47 39); Artaxi (tel: 01 42 08 50 50). If you call a taxi, the meter starts running when the driver gets the call. Extra charges are applied for luggage, train-station pick-up, and sometimes authorised rate hikes may be posted in the window. Three passengers is the limit, and cabbies are strict about this rule.

HOURS & HOLIDAYS

Banks have various hours *(see Money Matters on pages 87–89)*, generally from 9am–5pm Monday to Friday, with some branches closed at lunchtime, and/or on Monday; some open on Saturday.

The **Post Office** is open Monday to Friday from 8am–7pm and Saturday until noon (for branches with longer hours, *see Communications on page 94*).

Department stores open 9.30am–7pm, and close on Sunday. Many smaller shops close on Monday (especially food stores), and some close for lunch from about 1–3pm. Most shops are open until 7–8pm.

Public offices open 9am–5pm Monday to Friday, and sometimes Saturday morning. They are often closed noon–2pm.

ACCOMMODATION

There are many, many hotels in Paris, but it can be hard to find a room during busy periods. Your travel agent can probably book a room for you, otherwise reserve in advance. If you are booking on arrival, visit the Tourist Office on the Champs Elysées (Metro: Charles de Gaulle) or any of the main train stations except St Lazare. For a small fee they'll find you a room. Contact the hotels below to make a reservation. Breakfast is usually extra, from €6. Hotel tax costs up to around €1 per person per night in luxury hotels, less in unclassified hotels.

Deluxe Hotels

A double room with a bath costs at least €430 a night.

Crillon

10 Place de la Concorde (75008)
Tel: 01 44 71 15 00
Fax: 01 44 71 15 02
E-mail: crillon@crillon.com
Website: www.crillon.com
Some 160 rooms in a hotel on a wonderful site with views overlooking the River Seine. The hotel is next door to the American Embassy. The Crillon was extensively refurbished in the early 1980s; it has an excellent restaurant and air conditioning.

Above: a friendly taxi driver

Four Seasons George V

31 Av George V (75008)
Tel: 01 49 52 70 00
Fax. 01 49 52 70 20
E-mail: par.reservations@fourseasons.com
Website: www.fourseasons.com
This famous hotel is one of the largest in the city. Supremely elegant ambiance, and completely renovated for Christmas 1999. Has air-conditioning, of course, and a new swimming-pool and fitness centre.

InterContinental Paris

3 Rue de Castiglione (75001)
Tel: 01 44 77 11 11
Fax: 01 44 77 14 60
E-mail: paris@interconti.com
Website: www.interconti.com
With 445 rooms; excellent location, great service, all modern conveniences.

Lutetia

45 Blvd Raspail (75006)
Tel: 01 49 54 46 46
Fax: 01 49 54 46 00
E-mail: lutetia-paris@lutetia-paris.com
Website: www.lutetia-paris.com
The only Left Bank Palace located in the heart of St-Germain-des-Près. This beautiful 1930s style hotel has 250 air-conditioned Art Deco rooms, including 30 suites. The actress Catherine Deneuve is a regular visitor.

Meurice

228 Rue de Rivoli (75001)
Tel: 01 44 58 10 09
Fax: 01 44 58 10 78
E-mail: reservations@meuricehotel.com
Website: www.meuricehotel.com
After a magnificent two-year renovation, this lovely old building, nicknamed 'the Hotel of Kings', re-opens in April 2000, equipped with all modern conveniences and a new spa. It has 160 rooms.

Plaza-Athénée

25 Av Montaigne (75008)
Tel: 01 53 67 66 65
Fax: 01 53 67 66 66
Located near the Champs Elysées, this hotel has 190 sound-proofed rooms and suites. It also has restaurants, a disco and air conditioning, and was entirely renovated in 1999.

Raphaël

17 Av Kléber (75116)
Tel: 01 44 28 00 28
Fax: 01 45 01 21 50
E-mail: sales@raphael-hotel.com
A human-sized French Palace, located a stone's throw from Place de l'Etoile. The 86 rooms of this member of the 'Leading Small Hotels of the World' possess that unique ambiance of luxury and discretion.

Ritz

15 Place Vendôme (75001)
Tel: 01 43 16 30 30
Fax: 01 43 16 31 78
E-mail: resa@ritzparis.com
Website: www.ritzparis.com
Everything is perfect at the hotel that was the inspiration for the word 'ritzy'. There are some 175 rooms, good restaurants, spacious public rooms, all conveniences, air conditioning and secretarial services.

Expensive Hotels

For a double room with a bath in this grade of hotel you can expect to pay around €140–280.

Angleterre

44 Rue Jacob (75006)
Tel: 01 42 60 34 72
Fax: 01 42 60 16 93
E-mail: anglhotel@wanadoo.fr
Once the home of the British Ambassador, the Angleterre has 27 rooms, all with bath or shower. It has good service, traditional surroundings and a central location.

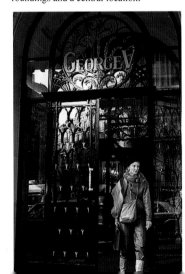

Right: the Four Seasons George V

Deux-Iles
59 Rue St Louis-en-L'Ile (75004)
Tel: 01 43 26 13 35
Fax: 01 43 29 60 25
This lovely 17th-century house has 17 rooms, all with bath or shower. It has a peaceful and friendly atmosphere.

Duc de Saint-Simon
14 Rue de St-Simon (75007)
Tel: 01 42 22 07 52
Fax: 01 45 48 68 25
E-mail: duc.de.saint.simon@wanadoo.fr
The charming hotel of the 7th *arrondissement.* Feel at home in one of the 34 rooms and suites overlooking the shady courtyard of this old residence.

Holiday Inn
10 Place de la République (75011)
Tel: 01 43 55 44 34
Fax: 01 47 00 32 34
E-mail: Holiday.Inn.paris.republique@ wanadoo.fr
One of several Holiday Inns in Paris. 318 rooms, all with bath or shower.

Montalembert
3 Rue de Montalembert (75007)
Tel: 01 45 49 68 68
Fax. 01 45 49 69 49
E-mail: welcome@hotel-montalembert.fr
Website: www.montalembert.com
Situated on the Left Bank, near Blvd St Germain and Musée d'Orsay, this historic landmark has been refurbished by decorator Christian Liaigre in a sober, smart and modern style. This elegant hotel has 51 rooms and 5 suites with all conveniences and air-conditioning.

Normandy
7 Rue de l'Echelle (75001)
Tel: 01 42 60 30 21
Fax: 01 42 60 45 81
E-mail: contact@normandyhotelparis.com
Website: www.normandyhotelparis.com
Has 115 rooms, all with bathrooms. Restaurant and bar. Comfortable and relaxing.

Relais S-Germain
9 Carrefour de l'Odéon (75006)
Tel: 01 43 29 12 05
Fax: 01 46 33 45 30
Fresh and French with its roof beams, 'Toile de Jouy' tapestries, antique furniture and exquisite breakfast baskets. The 22 bright rooms are air-conditioned and soundproofed, overlooking the Carrefour de l'Odéon at the crossroads of St-Germain-des-Près and the Latin Quarter. Four of them have a private kitchen for long stays. A real *hôtel de charme.*

Terrass
12–14 Rue Joseph-de-Maistre (75018)
Tel: 01 46 06 72 85
Fax: 01 42 52 29 11
E-mail: terrass@FranceNet.fr
Website: www.terrass-hotel.com
Montmartre hotel with 101 rooms, all with baths. Restaurant and bar, peaceful, relaxing location.

Above: a shady square in Montmartre

Moderate Hotels

One night in a double room will cost about €85–120. All the hotels listed here have fewer than 100 rooms; some will have bath/shower rooms and some will not.

Aramis

124 Rue de Rennes (75006)
Tel: 01 45 48 03 75
Fax: 01 45 44 99 29
The Aramis has 42 comfortable, attractive rooms with well-equipped bathrooms.

Buci Latin

34 Rue de Buci (75006)
Tel: 01 43 29 07 20
Fax: 01 43 29 67 44
In the style of Philippe Starck; and located in the very fashionable area of St-Germain.

Deux Iles

59 Rue St-Louis-en-l'Ile (75004),
Tel: 01 43 26 13 35
Fax: 01 43 29 60 25
Charming hotel in the heart of the Ile-St-Louis.

Grandes Ecoles

75 Rue du Cardinal Lemoine (75005)
Tel: 01 43 26 79 23
Fax: 01 43 25 28 15
E-mail: hotel.grandes.ecoles@wanadoo.fr
Website: www.hotel-grandes-ecoles.com
A pleasant hotel with a green garden and cobblestoned courtyard in the heart of Paris, behind the Panthéon, near the charming Place de la Contrescarpe. It has 51 rooms.

Lenox

9 Rue de l'Université (75007)
Tel: 01 42 96 10 95
Fax: 01 42 61 52 83
E-mail: lenox@gofornet.com
Website: www.lenoxsaintgermain.com
Charming and retro: photographers and models drop in here when in Paris. Book at least one month in advance, and avoid the fashion show periods (October and March).

Molière

21 Rue Molière (75001)
Tel: 01 42 96 22 01
Fax: 01 42 60 48 68
E-mail: moliere@worldnet.fr

Situated on a quiet street in the heart of Paris, near the Palais-Royal, the Louvre and the Opéra; charming, simple and comfortable. There are 32 air-conditioned rooms.

Louisiane

60 Rue de Seine (75006)
Tel: 01 43 29 59 30
Fax: 01 46 34 23 87
Overlooks the Buci market in St-Germain.

Hôtel Place des Vosges

12 Rue de Birague (75004)
Tel: 01 42 72 60 46
Fax: 01 42 72 02 64
Characterful, beautifully-renovated former stables. Only 16 rooms so book ahead.

Timhôtel

Tel: 01 44 15 81 15 (central number)
Fax: 01 44 15 95 26
Website: www.timhotel.fr
This reasonably priced chain has several 2–3-star hotels in town, all well-equipped (all rooms have a bath), small and centrally

located. Reservation recommended. American Express, Diners Club, Mastercard and Visa are accepted.

Inexpensive Hotels

Hotels that charge less than €60–75 a night for a double room with bath. Bear in mind that there may be a substantial difference in price between rooms with and without private bathrooms.

Esmeralda

4 Rue St Julien le Pauvre (75005)
Tel: 01 43 54 19 20
Fax: 01 40 51 00 68
Esmerelda has 19 rooms not far from Notre

Right: look out for this sign when choosing a hotel

Dame cathedral in the busy Latin Quarter. Credit cards are not accepted.

Montpensier
12 Rue de Richelieu (75001)
Tel: 01 42 96 28 50
Fax: 01 42 86 02 70
An excellent location for this 43-room hotel, near the Louvre and the Palais Royal.

Palais
2 Quai de la Mégisserie (75001)
Tel: 01 42 36 98 25
Fax: 01 42 21 41 67
A 19-room hotel near the Sainte Chapelle.

Palais Bourbon
49 Rue de Bourgogne (75007)
Tel: 01 45 51 63 32
Fax: 01 45 55 20 21
E-mail: htlbourbon@aol.com
Has 32 rooms with bath/shower. Small but modern; well situated for Les Invalides and the Rodin Museum.

Place des Vosges
12 Rue de Birague (75004)
Tel: 01 42 72 60 46
Fax: 01 42 72 02 64
All 16 rooms have bath or shower. It is situated in the Marais district. Pleasant, small and friendly – book well in advance. Credit cards are accepted.

St Jacques
35 Rue des Ecoles (75005)
Tel: 01 44 07 45 45
Fax: 01 43 25 65 50
An ordinary Parisian hotel, centrally located, with 35 rooms.

HEALTH & EMERGENCIES

If you lose your money, passport or other documents, or if they are stolen, look for the police station (*Commissariat*) nearest to the site of theft or loss, so that you can make an official declaration before reporting to the embassy of your country. You will need written police confirmation of theft or loss in order to make a claim on your insurance policy.

Useful contact numbers:
Ambulance (SAMU), *tel: 15*
Police Emergency, *tel: 17*
Fire Department, *tel: 18*
European Emergency, *tel:112*
Doctor *SOS Médecins, tel: 01 47 07 77 7*
American Hospital, *tel: 01 46 41 25 25*
Franco-British Hospital, *tel: 01 46 39 22 2*
British and American Pharmacy
1 Rue Auber (75009); Metro: Opera
8.30am–8pm Monday to Saturday, Englis spoken.

24-Hour Pharmacy: Dérhy
84 Avenue des Champs-Elysées (75008)
Metro: George V
English spoken

SOS-Help
English spoken
Crisis hotline: 01 47 23 80 80 from 3pm–11pm (subject to change).

COMMUNICATIONS

Post Offices
Post offices are open from 8am–7pm Monday to Friday, and many are open until noon or Saturday. They have distinctive yellow signs with a bird silhouette and the name *La Poste* The following branches have extended hours: **Poste Louvre** (52 Rue du Louvre, 75001 Metro: Louvre or Les Halles) is open 7 days a week, 24 hours a day; **Poste Paris 8** (71 Av des Champs Elysées, 75008, Metro: Franklin Roosevelt) is open 8am–10pm Mon-Sat, Sun 10am–noon and 2–8pm for mail only.

Telephones and Telegrams

There are public telephones in all post offices and booths on the street; a *café-tabac* has a telephone and most ordinary cafés have telephones for the use of customers. In cafés, you may have to buy a token (*jeton*) at the counter, or pay the cashier directly, or use a coin in the phone. Otherwise, most public phones now take *télécartes*, plastic cards, which are sold in denominations of 50 units and 120 units, available from tobacconists, post offices and approved vendors (carrying the sticker *Télécarte en vente ici*).

To call other countries, first dial the access code **00** followed by the national code: **Australia** (61); **Germany** (49); **Ireland** (353); **UK** (44); **US** and **Canada** (1). If using a US credit phone card, call the company's access number below: AT&T, tel: 00-0011; MCI, tel: 00-0019; Sprint, tel: 00-00874.

Telegrams can be sent from any Post Office. **Telefax** services are available at the Louvre Post Office (*see previous page*) and in most other branches.

Media and Bookshops

To keep on top of what's happening while you are in town, both *L'Officiel des Spectacles* and *Pariscope* publish an extensive list of restaurants, bars and clubs, concerts, plays and movies in town, information on museums, tours and sports, with opening hours, addresses and phone numbers.

American and British newspapers and magazines are available at many newsstands. For further English-language reading, try these major bookshops:

Brentano's
37 Av de l'Opéra (75002)
Metro: Opéra

Galignani
224 Rue de Rivoli (75001)
Metro: Tuileries

Shakespeare & Co
37 Rue de la Bûcherie (75005)
Metro: Cité

WH Smith
248 Rue de Rivoli (75001)
Metro: Concorde

MUSEUMS

The museums of Paris deserve all the praise lavished upon them. Check the *Officiel* magazine for current exhibitions and information on opening hours, which are subject to change. City of Paris museums close on Monday, national museums on Tuesday, and private museums may close on Tuesday or Friday. There are reductions for students, children under 18, and seniors, so bring identification if you fit any of these categories. Many national museums are free or half-price on Sunday. The **Carte Musées** (available from main Metro stations, museums, the tourist office and monuments) gives you access to over 70 museums and monuments in Paris (including the Louvre, Pompidou Centre, Picasso and Notre Dame…) for one, three or five days. Here are just a few of the many museums worth a visit:

Musée d'Art Moderne de la Ville de Paris
11 Av du Président Wilson (75016)
Metro: Alma-Marceau
Open Tuesday to Friday 10am–5.40pm, weekends until 6.45pm.
The period represented here falls between the Orsay and the Pompidou Centre: Post Impressionism up through Braque and Rouault. One wing houses the **Musée d'Art et d'Essai** (closed Tuesday).

Musée Delacroix
6 Rue de Furstenberg (75006)
Metro: St-Germain-des-Près
Open Wednesday to Monday 9.30am–12pm; 1.30–5pm.
Located on the exquisite Place Furstenberg, the studio and apartment of the famous 19th-century French painter. Drawings, paintings, sketches, letters and photographs introduce you to the intimate life of the artist.

Musée des Egouts de Paris
Pont de l'Alma (75007)
Metro: Alma-Marceau
Open Saturday to Wednesday 11am–5pm (till 4pm October–April). Closed part of January. Although this underground museum in the system itself is slightly smelly (and unsuitable for anyone likely to feel claustrophobic),

Left: keeping guard

it gives an interesting, entertaining overview of the system from the 1300s to today.

Musée Grévin
10 Blvd Montmartre (75009)
Metro: Rue Montmartre
Open daily 1–7pm (last tickets 6pm), from 10am in school holidays.
Late 19th-century characters and modern stars animate this waxworks museum. There are also some magic shows.

Musée Gustave Moreau
14 Rue de la Rochefoucauld (75009)
Metro: Trinité, St Georges
Open 10am–12.45pm, 2–5.15pm; Monday and Wednesday: 11am–5pm.
The family house of the 19th-century symbolist painter, with an exhibition of his works, among which are 5,000 drawings.

Musée Jacquemart-André
58 Blvd Haussmann (75008)
Metro: St Philippe-du-Roule
Open daily 10am–6pm.
Banker Edouard André had this lofty 'Hausmannian' residence designed to accommodate the works of art gathered by his wife and himself. Italian Renaissance paintings, Flemish masters and 18th century French School.

Musée Maillol
59/61 Rue de Grenelle (75007)
Metro: Rue du Bac

Open Wednesday to Monday 11am–6pm. This *hôtel particulier* in the Faubourg Saint-Germain displays the works of sculptor Aristide Maillol (1861–1944), whose statues adorn the Tuileries Garden – and of his friends, including Gauguin, Matisse, Cézanne and Degas. Good temporary exhibitions, usually featuring 20th-century art.

Musée de la Mode et du Textile, Musée des Arts Décoratifs
107 Rue de Rivoli (75001)
Metro: Palais Royal
Open 11am–6am. Closed Monday.
Within the Louvre building but with a separate entrance, these two museums are well worth a visit. The first presents the history of fashion from the 17th to the 20th centuries; the second displays beautifully crafted furniture, porcelain, crystal and *objets d'art*.

Musée Nissim de Camondo
63 Rue de Monceau (75008)
Metro: Villiers, Monceau
Open 10am–5am. Closed Monday, Tuesday.
A fine example of a Parisian *hôtel particulier*. Furnished by Count Moïse de Camondo, with an exceptional collection of 18th century paintings, furniture, rugs and porcelains.

Musée d'Orsay
1 Rue de Bellechasse (75007)
Metro: Solférino; RER: Orsay
Open 10am–6pm, from 9am Sunday and in summer, Thursday till 9.45pm (last entry 8pm). The long-abandoned Orsay train station in the centre of Paris was saved from destruction many years ago, but it wasn't given a new purpose until fairly recently. Preserving the building's *belle époque* architecture, Gae Aulenti redesigned the inner space into several exhibition levels, while keeping all the airy majesty of the original train station. Now it is devoted to works from the last half of the 19th century. One section, showing works by Delacroix and Ingres, leads up to the birth of Impressionism in the 1870s. Witness the changing aesthetics in works by Monet, Manet and Renoir. On the upper level are works by Van Gogh and Cézanne. Exhibitions in the two towers bring us up to the end of the century with Art Nouveau. Do not miss the opulent restaurant.

Above: the grand interior of the Musée d'Orsay

practical information

USEFUL INFORMATION

Children

There are several babysitting services in Paris; I suggest Kid Services (tel: 01 47 66 00 52) or Baby Prestige (tel: 01 53 53 02 02). Museums that are especially interesting to young travellers are Orsay (interactive computer terminals), Musée de la Marine, La Villette. There is a good children's library in the Pompidou Centre, suitable for older kids.

Kids aged 7–11 years can be left in the Jardin des Halles play area at the Forum des Halles while you shop. There are puppet theatres in the Luxembourg Gardens, in the Champs de Mars park next to the Eiffel Tower, and at the Rond Point des Champs Elysées.

A reduction for families (*Familles nombreuses*) is applied in some museums and for train fares at off-peak times. The booklet *Paris avec des yeux d'enfants*, free from tourist offices, lists Parisian attractions particularly suitable for children.

Students

Students must bring a valid student ID with a photo to be eligible for reductions at museums, theatres, etc. You can get more information on reductions at the Centre d'Information et Documentation Jeunesse (CIDJ), 101 Quai Branly (75015), tel: 01 44 49 12 00. Metro: Bir Hakeim.

Another useful address for young travellers is the *Accueil des Jeunes en France*, 119 Rue St Martin (75004). Metro: Rambuteau. They can help you find budget accommodation and suggest where you can meet like-minded people.

Disabled

Disabled travellers will have difficulty using public transport, and access to many older buildings is limited. There is a taxi service for people in wheelchairs, a special bus service for the disabled, and the Louvre museum offers tours for the handicapped.

The government publishes a booklet, *Touristes quand même*, which you can pick up in person at the French National Tourist Office, Parisian tourist offices, or from the Comité National Français de Liaison pour la Réadaptation des Handicapés, 236 Rue de Tolbiac (75007), tel: 01 53 80 66 66.

Senior Citizens

Senior citizens in Paris benefit from many reductions. To take advantage of them, you must provide proof of age, and in some cases (for reduced train fares) a passport-sized photo which is affixed to a discount card.

Tourist Offices

The main tourist office is at 127 Avenue des Champs Elysées (75008), Metro: Charles de Gaulle-Etoile (tel: 08 36 68 31 12). There are also branches in Carrousel du Louvre (01 42 44 10 50), Tour Eiffel (01 45 51 22 15), Gare du Nord (01 45 26 94 82), Gare de Lyon (01 43 43 33 24), Roissy CDG (01 48 62 27 29), Orly (01 49 75 00 90). Website: www.paris-touristoffice.com

EMBASSIES & CONSULATES

Australia, 4 Rue Jean-Rey (75015) tel: 01 40 59 33 00
Canada, 35 Avenue Montaigne (75008) tel: 01 44 43 29 00
Ireland, 4 Rue Rude (75016) tel: 01 44 17 67 00
New Zealand, 7 Rue Léonard-de-Vinci, (75016), tel: 01 45 00 24 11
UK, 35 Rue du Faubourg St Honoré (75008) tel: 01 44 51 31 00.
USA, 2 Rue St-Florentin (75001) tel: 01 43 12 22 22

Right: dancing on the Pont des Arts

credits

ACKNOWLEDGEMENTS

8/9, 38	**Ping Amranand**
4B, 31B, 32, 35, 37, 39, 41B, 43T, 47, 49 52B, 53, 55, 56, 58, 67, 68, 69, 70, 71, 87	**Guy Bourdier**
Back cover, 1, 6T, 6B, 7T, 7B, 11, 14B, 16 20, 21, 22, 23, 25, 26, 27T, 27B, 29, 30, 1T, 33, 34, 36T, 36B, 42, 43B, 44, 45, 46, 48, 51, 52T, 54, 57, 59, 60, 61T, 61B, 62, 63T, 63B, 64T, 64B, 72, 73, 74T, 74B, 75, 76, 77, 78, 79, 80, 81, 82, 83T, 83B, 85, 86, 88, 89, 90 91, 92, 93, 94, 96, 97, 98	**Annabel Elston**
66	**IAURIF, Paris**
5	**Catherine Karnow**
12, 13T, 15T	**Musées de la Ville de Paris**
13B	**Photo Bibliothèque Nationale, Paris**
10	**Steve Van Beek**
2/3, 24T, 28, 41T, 50, 65, 84	**Bill Wassman**
Front cover	**Pictures Colour Library**
Cartography	**Mike Larby**

© APA Publications GmbH & Co. Verlag KG Singapore Branch, Singapore

Left: taking a break in the Quartier Latin

INSIGHT
Pocket Guides

Insight Pocket Guides pioneered a new approach to guidebooks, introducing the concept of the authors as "local hosts" who would provide readers with personal recommendations, just as they would give honest advice to a friend who came to stay. They also included a full-size pull-out map.

Now, to cope with the needs of the 21st century, new editions in this growing series are being given a new look to make them more practical to use, and restaurant and hotel listings have been greatly expanded.

Also from Insight Guides...

Insight Guides is the classic series, providing the complete picture with expert and informative text and stunning photography. Each book is an ideal travel planner, a reliable on-the-spot companion – and a superb visual souvenir of a trip. 193 titles.

Insight Maps are designed to complement the guidebooks. They provide full mapping of major destinations, and their laminated finish gives them ease of use and durability. 65 titles.

Insight Compact Guides are handy reference books, modestly priced yet comprehensive. The text, pictures and maps are all cross-referenced, making them ideal books to consult while seeing the sights. 119 titles.

INSIGHT POCKET GUIDE TITLES

Aegean Islands	California,	Israel	Moscow	Seville, Cordoba &
Algarve	Northern	Istanbul	Munich	Granada
Alsace	Canton	Jakarta	Nepal	Seychelles
Amsterdam	Chiang Mai	Jamaica	New Delhi	Sicily
Athens	Chicago	Kathmandu Bikes	New Orleans	Sikkim
Atlanta	Corsica	& Hikes	New York City	Singapore
Bahamas	Costa Blanca	Kenya	New Zealand	Southeast England
Baja Peninsula	Costa Brava	Kuala Lumpur	Oslo and	Southern Spain
Bali	Costa Rica	Lisbon	Bergen	Sri Lanka
Bali Bird Walks	Crete	Loire Valley	Paris	Sydney
Bangkok	Denmark	London	Penang	Tenerife
Barbados	Fiji Islands	Los Angeles	Perth	Thailand
Barcelona	Florence	Macau	Phuket	Tibet
Bavaria	Florida	Madrid	Prague	Toronto
Beijing	Florida Keys	Malacca	Provence	Tunisia
Berlin	French Riviera	Maldives	Puerto Rico	Turkish Coast
Bermuda	(Côte d'Azur)	Mallorca	Quebec	Tuscany
Bhutan	Gran Canaria	Malta	Rhodes	Venice
Boston	Hawaii	Manila	Rome	Vienna
Brisbane & the	Hong Kong	Marbella	Sabah	Vietnam
Gold Coast	Hungary	Melbourne	St. Petersburg	Yogjakarta
British Columbia	Ibiza	Mexico City	San Francisco	Yucatán Peninsula
Brittany	Ireland	Miami	Sarawak	
Brussels	Ireland's	Montreal	Sardinia	
Budapest	Southwest	Morocco	Scotland	

INDEX